INNOCENT BLOOD

*Challenging the Powers of Death with th
Gospel of Life*

John Ensor
Cruciform Press | Released September, 2c

To John Cissel.
A man of integrity, generosity, and brotherly love.
A partner with me in the good works God prepared
for us to do together starting twenty years ago.
A friend dedicated to the principle that the fragrance
of Christ in us should emanate outward as
the very aroma of life. Thank you.
– John Ensor

CruciformPress

"God's Word tells us to be prepared to give an answer to everyone who asks us a reason for the hope within us, and it also tells us that we should do this with gentleness and respect. This book does just that. With decades of experience and true wisdom, John Ensor beautifully shows us how our glorious God delights in our courageous fight for the innocent, and that he commands us to fight, not with the words and weapons of man but with the living and active Gospel of Jesus Christ as we depend on the Holy Spirit to change hearts, renew minds, and protect the innocent—for the sake of the precious innocent of all ages and for the incomparable glory of God for eternity."

Burk Parsons, associate pastor, Saint Andrew's; Editor, *Tabletalk*

"*Innocent Blood* brings Christians face to face with the horror of abortion and our responsibility to intervene. Better yet, by showing how our activism is to be motivated and fueled by the gospel, Ensor challenges us to devote our lives to magnifying Jesus Christ through seeking justice for the unborn."

Trevin Wax, author of *Counterfeit Gospels* and *Holy Subversion*, editor at LifeWay Christian Resources

"*Innocent Blood* is a powerful indictment of those responsible for the abortion holocaust and those who have not joined in attempts to stop it. The author presents many biblical passages that should constrain our consciences and our actions. There are areas of theology about which sincere Christians can disagree, but this is not one of them. The Scriptures are as clear as they can be that God's people have the responsibility to stop the shedding of innocent blood."

John Frame, Professor of Systematic Theology and Philosophy, Reformed Theological Seminary

"Stellar! John Ensor provides a bridge between the defense of innocent human life and the proclamation of the gospel. His concisely worded thesis is theologically grounded, philosophically sound, and gives pastors the tools to engage the culture on the burning moral question of our day. I wholeheartedly recommend this book!"

Scott Klusendorf, Speaker and author of *The Case for Life: Equipping Christians to Engage the Culture* (Crossway)

CruciformPress
something new in Christian publishing

Our Books: Short. Clear. Concise. Helpful. Inspiring. Gospel-focused. *Print; ebook formats: Mobi, ePub, PDF.*

Consistent Prices: Every book costs the same.

Subscription Options: Print books or ebooks delivered to you on a set schedule, at a discount. Or buy print books or ebooks individually.

Pre-paid or Recurring Subscriptions

Print Book	$6.49 each
Ebook	$3.99 each

Non-Subscription Sales

1-5 Print Books	$8.45 each
6-50 Print Books	$7.45 each
More than 50 Print Books	$6.45 each
Single Ebooks (bit.ly/CPebks)	$5.45 each

CruciformPress.com

Innocent Blood: Challenging the Powers of Death with the Gospel of Life

Print ISBN:	978-1-936760-29-9
ePub ISBN:	978-1-936760-30-5
Mobipocket ISBN:	978-1-936760-31-2

Table of Contents

Lest Innocent Blood Be Shed 7
Introduction and Summary

Chapters

One   *Blood-Precious* 19
Christ Died for the Innocent

Two   *Blood-Guilt*. 37
God's Response to the Shedding of Innocent
Blood

Three   *Blood-Atonement*. 59
Christ's Provision for the Shedding of Innocent
Blood

Four   *Blood-Earnest*. 71
Christ's Courage to Stop the Shedding of
Innocent Blood

Five   *Blood-War*. 93
Satan's Plan to Delay the Final Triumph of the
Gospel

Appendix
Six Things You Can Do to Help Save the
Innocent. 113
Endnotes 116

More books from Cruciform Press. 121

LEST INNOCENT BLOOD BE SHED

Introduction and Summary

This book takes its cue from Deuteronomy 19:7-10.

> Therefore I command you, You shall set apart three cities. And if the LORD your God enlarges your territory, as he has sworn to your fathers, and gives you all the land that he promised to give to your fathers…then you shall add three other cities to these three, lest innocent blood be shed in your land that the LORD your God is giving you for an inheritance, and so the guilt of bloodshed be upon you.

Here, God commands his people to take extensive precautions and invest significant effort, even to the point of establishing cities, in order to avoid three terrible results:

1. The shedding of innocent blood
2. The resulting bloodguilt
3. The judgments of the Lord implied in the term *bloodguilt*

The clear principle set forth in this passage is also developed throughout Scripture by numerous commands and examples—God's people are called to prevent both the death of innocents and the bloodguilt that results. The purpose of this book is to explore, explain, and urge our obedience to this call.

In what ways have God's people taken this principle to heart and lived it out? Where they have been successful, how did they find the courage to prevent the shedding of innocent blood? These are some of the key questions explored in the following chapters.

Finally, at the end of the book, I flip the script. Instead of trying to understand the will of God and calling us to be faithful in it, I look at the matter of shedding innocent blood and bloodguilt from Satan's perspective. I have never spent much time trying to understand the mind of the Evil One. In doing so here I only seek to be faithful to what God has revealed about our adversary in Scripture on this matter.

What I have discovered is sobering, indeed – *Satan sees the connection between rescuing the innocent and bringing Good News to the guilty. Most Christians do not.*

Few of us today even take the time to consider whether such a connection might exist. Too many of us think, or simply assume, that rescuing the innocent and bringing Good News to the guilty are separate issues. Satan knows they are not separate. The people I present in this book know they are *distinct* issues, but not *separable* issues. These men and women represent a remarkable Christian heritage, a heritage in which courage is exercised and sacrifice is embraced in order to prevent the shedding of innocent blood. My hope is that something in the following pages will spur on courageous, cross-bearing labor—labor that can turn this heritage into a legacy for the next generation.

Lest Innocent Blood Be Shed

One of the well-marked books in my library is *Lest Innocent Blood Be Shed*. The author, Phillip Hallie, writes, "During the four years of the German occupation of France, the village of Le Chambon, with a population of about 3,000 impoverished people, saved the lives of about 5,000 Jewish refugees. Most of them were children." [1]

I read this story for the first time nearly thirty years ago. I recently pulled it off my shelf to reread. I was stunned to see how heavily marked it was in my own handwriting: "Take note!", "Our moral obligation," "cf. Proverbs 24," "Saw themselves as faithful," "Living out PGS" (Parable of the Good Samaritan). I was digging out of their story something I was also observing in Scripture—there are occasions when courage is required of our faith.

As Christians, we all know this in a general way. We love to tell the stories of those who proved faithful to God's call and gave themselves to courageous living in spite of opposition and want. The men of Issachar are described as those "who had understanding of the times, to know what Israel ought to do" (1 Chronicles 12:32). There have always been a few people like these, people who understood the challenges of their own day and how God would have them respond.

The problem with quoting historical examples, such as the rescuers of Jews in the village of Le Chambon, is that it is easy to see *now* what was at stake *then*. Everyone today can see how the faithful ones back then were marked by their courage. Everyone today can dismiss the moral cowardice and compromise of those who passively accepted what should have been openly and courageously opposed.

I do not want to write a book that effectively has me standing on the corner with my arms raised, praying, "I thank you, Father, that I am not like those morally blind and cowardly leaders of the past." Historical examples only have value if they produce self-examination. So we must ask, what is the inviolable principle that moved the people of Le Chambon to give so much, risk so much, and in some cases lose everything in order to be faithful to God's command? In what form is this same principle under attack today? How must we fight the same battle as it is being reconstituted on our own watch? In this matter, is our theology and its application truly attuned to the specific circumstances of the present generation?

But then we must probe our hearts and our theology further. Do we hold theologically elaborate, well-reasoned positions today that, in truth, simply protect and preserve a job, a position, the status quo? Does the theology that truly controls our life choices and daily actions summon us to cross-bearing labor? Or to something decidedly more self-focused? That is, are we keen to learn from Scripture and history when courage is demanded of *our* faith?

My Purpose and My Plea

My *purpose* in this book is to examine present-day situations in which courage is required of our faith, lest innocent blood be shed. These situations can arise seemingly by happenstance, by an escalation of tensions, or by public policy.

My *plea* is that whenever we encounter such a situation we resolve not to accept it, rationalize it, bury it under allegedly higher priorities, or pretend we do not know it is happening. Instead, like those who came before us and who are commended for their faithfulness, may we fight the shedding of innocent blood with all our moral might and practical effort, on the spot and for the long haul.

This plea gathers its force from four convictions:

1. God presents the prevention of the shedding of innocent blood as a matter of highest priority.
2. As Christians, we have accepted a false choice between the temporal value of human life and the eternal value.
3. There is a unique courage that comes from faith.
4. The shedding of innocent blood is and has always been central to the fierce and desperate strategy of the Enemy.

The Priority of Prevention

God always presents the shedding of innocent blood to his people as a matter of the highest priority. It comes to us in a way that knocks us off stride (or ought to). It messes with our schedules. It is arresting. It interrupts our normal patterns, at least temporarily. When life-saving actions are required to prevent the shedding of innocent blood, it falls particularly upon us, who believe, to suffer the imposition and take whatever preventive steps are necessary, lest innocent blood be shed and bloodguilt stain us all.

Some years ago, rapid spring melting led to massive flooding along the Mississippi in the Quad cities area of Illinois and Iowa. Homes, farmland, livestock, and people were all in danger. My mother called to tell me she was dropping everything to drive west about 150 miles to help fill sandbags. The woman was almost 70! She was not going to be stopped. I thought, "Something bad could happen to her." Then I reflected on how much Christ had changed her life and realized that this was normative risky behavior for someone who has come to love God and neighbor. If trouble comes by such behavior, it is the kind of trouble that glorifies God and the gospel. She did fine.

The kinds of actions needed to preserve human life are interruptive by nature. That is how you can tell in a particular circumstance when someone values life—that person is willing to be interrupted to protect it. In most cases, we can easily tweak and juggle things so that the death of others, or the threat of their death, does not impact us directly. We can maneuver like this because the innocents in danger are often powerless people, marginal actors on the social scene, rarely the kind of people who can force our attention or compel a change of plans. They are hardly ever personal friends or potential partners, contributors, or clients—should *these* people come into the cross-hairs of death, no word from God is needed to compel us to look out for them.

This raises a vital point: *The commands of Scripture exist that we might be compelled to do what does not come naturally.*

The innocents whom God has commanded us to care about are precisely the kind of people we are apt to overlook—and would *prefer* to overlook. The psalmist states plainly, "Maintain the rights of the *afflicted* and the *destitute*. Rescue the *weak* and the *needy*; deliver them from the hand of the wicked" (Psalm 82:3-4). These people have little or no claim on our love or kindness. Their problems are not personal to us. They are usually strangers. But they are *personal* friends of our God. In their plight they have cried out to God for help. He has heard their cry. In response, God calls *us* to look for them and drop everything, if need be, to come to their aid. Lest innocent blood be shed.

The False Choice

My second conviction arises out of a false choice I see blowing in the wind. We who love God, cherish the gospel, and affirm the *ultimate* value of one's eternal life (soul) must never, never, never neglect life's *temporal* value. A biblically based, cross-centered commitment does not lead to a focus on eternal life at the expense of mortal life. It values both, each in their own way. If you see them in an either/or dynamic, consider how this is a false choice.

If the shedding of innocent blood is not truly of central concern to us, then neither can the cross of Christ be our supreme concern. After all, w*hat is it that elevates the cross to supreme importance? The shedding of innocent blood.*

This false choice between eternal life and temporal life is not just unbiblical. It is deeply unattractive. In the Parable of the Good Samaritan, Jesus describes how the Priest, the Levite, and the Samaritan are all, in turn, confronted by the same instance of innocent blood being shed. The actions of the first two are distasteful, repugnant, offensive to the law of love. Love does more than bemoan murder. It stops it by all practical effort.

When we stand witness to people, who claim to love God, ignoring the shedding of innocent blood in favor of "more important" things, Jesus doesn't want us just to point out that it's wrong. He wants us to feel something. He wants us to be morally offended.

Loving God and loving neighbor are not separate choices. One flows sweetly from the other. Loving my neighbor will always mean a desire to help him or her find the grace of God in all its manifestations. Loving my neighbor will occasionally arrest me, and maybe even require me to help prevent someone from being murdered. Loving God and loving neighbor are never at odds with each other. Those who try to do one at the expense of the other offend both God and neighbor. I hope to prove this.

The Courage That Comes from Faith

The third conviction behind my plea is that the courage needed to oppose, if not stop, the shedding of innocent blood (suffering in the process, if necessary), is not something *besides* faith or *other than* faith or *in addition* to faith. It is a courage that *flows from* faith and is *produced by* faith. Believing in God works. By this I mean that belief in God produces good works. And one of the good works that faith itself generates is cross-bearing courage to rescue the innocent.

This kind of courage, which is actually just faith acting under pressure, is also attractive and winsome to others. Christians down through the ages have known this is true. We write about it all the time. We herald it. We have been wooed and won by those who demonstrate it. When we are not writing or reading real stories of righteous, God-glorifying courage, we are making them up in novels.

I dare you to read Hebrews 11:35-38 with fresh eyes and not experience the beauty of courage toward God.

> Some were tortured, refusing to accept release, so that they might rise again to a better life. Others suffered mocking and flogging, and even chains and imprisonment. They were stoned, they were sawn in two, they were killed with the sword. They went about in skins of sheep and goats, destitute, afflicted, mistreated — of whom the world was not worthy — wandering about in deserts and mountains, and in dens and caves of the earth.

Where does such strength come from? Where, for example, did the midwives of Egypt find the courage to defy the law of the land and refuse to shed innocent blood? Where did Rahab find the courage to rescue the spies at risk to her life? Gideon, Samuel, the prophets and others "enforced justice" (Hebrews 11:33). Where

did they get the courage to do this? "*By faith*, Rahab…
welcomed the spies" (Hebrews 11:31). "*Through faith…*
they enforced justice." There is a courage required of our
faith and supplied through our faith.

The reason this is important is that when you are
confronted with a situation in which a lack of action will
result in the shedding of innocent blood and bloodguilt,
you never know if your intervention will succeed or get
you in trouble. That is why faith demands courage. Some
were enabled to shut the mouths of lions (Hebrews 11:33).
Others were sawn in two (Hebrews 11:37). Bad things
can happen when you follow Christ. But they are bad
things that are good for you. Avoiding them means that
good things that are bad for you may be preserved. To me,
that appears to be the take-away lesson of Hebrews 11.

When you entrust your life to Christ and to his safe-
keeping, you can afford to risk it. This is why I say that
courage is *required* or *demanded* of us who have saving
faith. Thankfully, looking to God is how God supplies
us the courage we need to be faithful. To be precise, it is
not that we need faith plus courage. We simply need the
courage that faith in God produces. As water can turn to
ice, faith in God can turn into life-saving, death-defying
action. Lest innocent blood be shed.

The Designs of Our Adversary

The fourth conviction giving rise to my plea comes from
a trembling look at the enemy's plans. Our adversary,
the Devil, has a gospel-centered plan as well—he is fully
committed to stopping its progress! He must stop the

spread of the gospel and delay the fulfillment of the Great Commission to delay his own day of judgment (Revelation 12:12).

One of his primary weapons of choice is the blunt instrument of child-killing—the most heinous form of the shedding of innocent blood. Look at how Satan has acted down through history.

In Egypt. Not knowing whom God had elected to deliver Israel out of bondage, Satan employed the brutal weapon of mass child-killing to try to snuff out the life and work of Moses (Exodus 1).

In the Promised Land. Satan enticed Israel into child-sacrifice (Psalm 106: 37-38) in a way that seemed to make God a perverse partner in the offense, for it was done in the name of pleasing God. I suspect Satan was trying to trap God in his righteousness, forcing him to destroy his own people out of his righteous indignation and thus destroy the work of redemption.

At the incarnation. The inconsolable mothers of Bethlehem also bear witness that Satan was willing to use the blunt instrument of mass child-killing in his attempt to devour the One Child before he could grow up to rule as both Savior and Lord.

In our midst. Satan continues to wield the same weapon today, devouring as many innocents as possible in an attempt to kill those who would otherwise grow up to advance and complete the cause of Christ among every tribe and tongue and nation (Revelation 12:17).

So there you go. I have spilled the beans on all my conclusions. I have given you a few of the biblical markers that have led me down this path. As this book continues, you will see that I have found both glorious and shameful examples that add light to that path. These examples lead to places that will make you squirm (at least, they made me squirm) and put everything to the test.

Will you look at the shedding of innocent blood in our midst today and find the courage, the courage that flows from faith, to run to the point of the spear?

That is my invitation to you as you continue with this book.

ONE
BLOOD-PRECIOUS

Christ Died for the Innocent

From oppression and violence he redeems their life,
and precious is their blood in his sight. — *Psalm 72:1*

There are no important divisions between human beings. The
main distinction among people is between those who believe that
those in need are as precious as they themselves are, and those
who do not believe this. [2] — *André Trocmé*

The work that Christ accomplished on the cross is far more extensive than we often imagine. Christ did not only die for the guilty. He died for the innocent.

Consider Psalm 72. In verse 14, the Psalmist looks to the suffering and death of the innocent and says, "Precious is their blood in his sight." When *blood* is used this way in Scripture it refers to human life in the flesh, this temporary phase when our eternal being is housed in a mortal body. That life is precious to God. The same Psalm tells us that God "delivers the needy when he calls…He has pity on the weak…and saves the lives of the needy. From oppression and violence he redeems their life" (72:12-14). Christians rightly look to and rely on promises like these from Scripture all the time. So it is only proper to ask, *how* does God deliver, save, and redeem the lives of people from oppression and violence?

The direct means he uses from one situation to the next may vary widely but the unifying factor, the underlying reality that makes it all possible, is the same in each case. God delivers, saves, and redeems, whether temporally or eternally, because of and through the cross.

Christ died for the innocent. Think it through with me.

The Power of the Cross for Temporal Salvation

By *innocent*, I don't mean sinless before God. All of us are guilty before a holy God. I mean harmless, pure, or free from guilt before our fellow man or the laws of man. Babies and little children come to mind first when we speak of the innocent in this sense; they are harmless and without guile. But adults, too, are called innocent when they have done nothing wrong toward their neighbor. To punish them without due process, or on the basis of a false report, or because they are poor and have no proper defenders, or to please the wealthy or powerful, is to harm the *innocent*. So we read in Exodus 23:6-7, "You shall not pervert the justice due to your poor in his lawsuit. Keep far from a false charge, and do not kill the *innocent* and righteous, for I will not acquit the wicked." Rather, justice requires judges to acquit the *innocent* and condemn the guilty (Deuteronomy 25:1). And again, "Woe to those who… acquit the guilty for a bribe, and deprive the innocent of his right!" (Isaiah 5:22-23). And finally, murder itself, since it represents the unlawful taking of human life, is called the shedding of *innocent* blood. Bloodguilt is God's term of indictment for the shedding of innocent blood, and is usually expressed in Scripture as the "guilt of bloodshed" or the "guilt of innocent blood."

To return to our question, therefore, *how* does God save the innocent from oppression and violence?

The cross is God's primary means of accomplishing everything in history. All of God's purposes find their holy impulse emanating from the cross of Christ. Even the goodness and mercy of God that is extended in no small measure to all of creation (this is what theologians call common grace) flows from the cross. All of God's purposes regarding the weak, the innocent, and the oppressed are connected to the cross and flow from the cross—even if the weak, innocent, and oppressed aren't Christians and will never become Christians. So, when I say Christ died for the innocent, I mean his death secured gifts of *temporal* deliverance (that is, in this life) for the weak and the innocent as well as *eternal* deliverance from our sin before God.

Please do not hear me suggesting that the immediate focus of the cross is anything but our guilt before God. The apostle Paul calls it a matter of first importance that we understand "Christ died for our sins" (1 Corinthians 15:3). Christ's immediate view was suffering the just and full punishment due for each and all of our sins. All I am pleading for is that we also see that beyond this reconciling gift of substitutionary atonement, Christ saw multiple other gifts, resplendent in their own way, purchased by his blood. For now, I will just emphasize two of these: a clean conscience and a sacrificial heart.

A clean conscience. In paying for our sins, Jesus satisfied the just wrath of a righteous God (Romans 5:9). This satisfaction secured a reconciling peace that flows back and forth between a holy God and those made holy through the work of the cross (Romans 5:1). That means Christ also died in part to cleanse our consciences. To be reconciled to God means we are fully convinced that Christ paid the full price due and that therefore nothing prevents us from drawing near to God (Hebrews 10:22).

A sacrificial heart. Christ died to grant us the life-changing work of the Holy Spirit and the endowment of many gifts that enable us to serve him. When Christ went to the cross, he saw how his death included the gift of regeneration by his Spirit, which would turn our hearts from ones that couldn't care less about our neighbors into ones that are moved to sacrificial and life-preserving work (John 14:12). Christ died to make us look at the Good Samaritan and say, "I will go and do likewise."

The Examples of Le Chambon and Job

God answered the pleas of women and children in the village of Le Chambon, France, who were fleeing death in the 1940s. He did it by dying on the cross for those in Le Chambon who believed, and by his Spirit turning those believers into death-defying Samaritans. Those innocent women and children would not have been rescued in 1943 if Christ had not had them also in mind in AD 33. Precious was their blood in his sight, before they were even born.

The cross is behind tens of thousands of deliverance-and-rescue stories that have unfolded down through the ages in every culture. Even going back to ancient times, God heard the cries of the poor and rescued the innocent from the wicked in anticipation of his work on the cross. Job said of himself,

> I delivered the poor who cried for help, and the fatherless who had none to help him. The blessing of him who was about to perish came upon me, and I caused the widow's heart to sing for joy. I put on righteousness, and it clothed me; my justice was like a robe and a turban. I was eyes to the blind and feet to the lame. I was a father to the needy, and I searched out the cause of him whom I did not know. I broke the fangs of the unrighteous and made him drop his prey from his teeth (29:12-17).

The blind need borrowed eyes. The lame need borrowed feet. When you are caught in the fangs of the unrighteous, you will cry out for deliverance and hope that God sends a rescuer. Job was such a rescuer.

Job was rich in mercy toward all these people because God was first rich in mercy toward Job. God did this gracious work in Job on behalf of the blind, the lame, and those about to be devoured, in spite of the fact that Job, too, was sinful and under his wrath. Nonetheless, God did this work of grace in and through Job. He did so based on the same work of Christ on the cross that lies at the foundation of our own good works.

Do not get hung up on the fact that Job lived thousands of years before Christ. You and I live thousands of years after Christ. For God, time does not only flow in one direction. The cross justifies grace and transforms lives in both directions — after Christ and before Christ. Job (along with Abraham, Moses, David, and others) was saved and transformed by faith in the *hope* of atonement (19:25-26). We experience the same salvation and transformation by faith in the *fulfillment* of atonement. Either way we can say that we love our neighbors because Christ first loved us. [3] Telescoping the timing, Job lent his eyes to the blind and his feet to the lame, and he snatched the innocent from the jaws of death, because Christ died on the cross for Job.

Our Superior Position: God's Valuation of Human Life

In stressing how Christ died for the innocent, I am trying to express the emphasis in Scripture on the value of human life itself. If the Holy Spirit had inspired the writers of Scripture to express emphasis with a yellow highlighter, we would see our first yellow mark early in Genesis: "And God saw everything that he had made, and behold, it was *very* good" (1:31). God created the earth and the seas, and declared it good (1:10). He created the sun and the moon, each to rule in their own way, and

called it good (1:18). Then he created man and woman—
human life—and he declared the whole package *very*
good. Not until humanity was present in creation did
good become *very* good, and that *very* is equivalent to a
yellow highlighter mark.

Human life is what God values most among everything he has made. Jesus said it this way: "You are of *more
value* than many sparrows" (Matthew 10:31). "More value"
according to whom? Jesus spoke God's own opinion here—
the objective, ultimate truth about the value of human beings.

I hope it makes you glad that God values your life as
a human being above everything else in creation. It makes
me glad. I know it made David very glad because he
rejoiced at the thought:

> When I look at your heavens, the work of your
> fingers, the moon and the stars, which you have set in
> place, what is man that you are mindful of him, and
> the son of man that you care for him? Yet you have
> made him a little lower than the heavenly beings and
> crowned him with glory and honor. You have given
> him dominion over the works of your hands; you
> have put all things under his feet. (Psalm 8:3-6)

Valued Because We Share His Image

In what sense is mankind crowned with glory and honor?
Why are we of much more value than many sparrows?
The Christian answer, uniformly affirmed throughout the
ages, is that human life is precious to God because we are
made in his image. "God created man in his *own image*,

in the image of God he created him; male and female he created them" (Genesis 1:27).

This metaphysical assertion—that all people, male and female, are created in God's own image—explains the entire history of courageous Christianity. It is conceived in the words *created in his image*. This is what gives human life *intrinsic* value, not just utilitarian value. Each human life, individually, is more valuable than many sparrows.

Abraham believed this. The midwives of Egypt believed this. Rahab believed this. James believed this, which is why he said we must not even curse, let alone kill, our fellow man (James 3:9). Every person commended for faith and courage in Hebrews 11 believed this. All the patriarchs, prophets, apostles, and disciples believed this. Every person you admire for their Christian faith today believes this.

If we took this reality to heart, we could end the book here and turn the world upside down.

The Christian Application of Man's Valuation

The intrinsic value of every human life is the first truth and the primary impulse that explains why Christianity works so hard in the care of human life. Christianity was birthed into the cruelty of pagan Rome where human life was held in low esteem. Violent death was offered as public entertainment. Abortion, infanticide, exposure, and abandonment were part of the culture. But every- where Christianity grows, it acts like Job when it comes to the death of innocents. It breaks the fangs of the unrighteous and makes him drop his prey from his teeth (Job 29:17). Here are just a few examples of how Christians have effected gospel-centered change by responding to the world around them.[4]

The young and helpless. Christianity creates orphanages and promotes adoption. In these recent times, Christianity has created the pregnancy-help movement.

The elderly and sick. Because life has intrinsic value, not just utilitarian value, Christianity views the elderly and the sick as objects of care rather than as disposable items. So Christianity made taking care of parents in their old age a fundamental exercise of love (1 Timothy 5:8). Christians developed nursing care and hospice care. Christians invented hospitals and created the first emergency hotline. Christian faith drove us to understand disease and look for cures. It has always opposed the policies and practices of human eugenics and euthanasia.

The oppressed. The intrinsic value of human life led Christians to improve the rights and dignity of women. It elevates human sexuality and works even today to deliver women and men out of sex trafficking. It decried slavery so hard and so long that institutionalized slavery is now gone forever. Out of the dust of slavery's collapse, the intrinsic value for human life promoted education for everyone. It demanded fair labor laws and codified human rights in constitutions worldwide. It still does, for human beings made in God's image are yet oppressed in many parts of the world today.

The suffering. Belief in the intrinsic value of human life has created innumerable ministries to the poor, the homeless, the alcoholic and drug-addicted, the prostitute, the mentally ill, the blind, refugees fleeing war, and immigrants fleeing poverty.

There are many good ministries committed to the various ways in which we might care for the rest of creation, but why has the history of Christianity been so consistently and radically consumed with the welfare of the innocent and helpless? Because our fellow man is *more valuable* than many sparrows.

You may say that much of these good works were motivated by the gospel, a love of Christ, and a passion to make his saving grace known throughout the world. I agree! All of these glorious efforts flow from the cross. Indeed, Christ died for the innocent. All of these are part of the "good works, which God prepared beforehand, that we should walk in them" (Ephesians 2:10).

Life Is of God

If the gospel motivates Christians to do good works, what motivated God to bring forth the gospel in the first place? His intrinsic love of human life and his sovereign choice to be glorified in the gift of life.

God is life. He breathes "the breath of life" (Genesis 2:7) and "he is your life" (Deuteronomy 30:20). He says, "Whoever finds me finds life" (Proverbs 8:35).

God gives life. "In his hand is the life of every living thing and the breath of all mankind" (Job 12:10).

God loves life. He upholds life (Psalm 54:4), preserves life (Genesis 45:5), and restores life (Ruth 4:15). God is "the light of life" (Job 33:30) and the keeper of life

(Psalm 121:7), the "fountain of life" (Proverbs 14:27) and the redeemer of life (Psalm 72:14).

Pursuing him is "the path of life" (Psalm 16:11), fearing him prolongs life (Proverbs 10:27), and living in unity before him is "life forevermore" (Psalm 133:3)! Therefore we cry with the psalmist:

- Give me life according to your word! (119:25)
- Give me life according to your promise! (119:154)
- Give me life according to your rules. (119:156)
- Give me life according to your steadfast love. (119:159)

Our Common Position: Life Is in the Blood

The well-being of mankind rests upon the truth that because human life is made in God's image, it is chief among God's affections when it comes to his creation. This is true despite the fact that we do not know precisely what it means to be made in God's image. A number of reasonable suggestions have been offered, and I am persuaded that at least part of the answer is found in David's words, "You have given him dominion over the works of your hands; you have put all things under his feet" (Psalm 8:3-6).

God is sovereign and rightly rules over all things. In creating man in his image, he made us to rule over the rest of creation (Genesis 1:28). At the same time, God gave us some common ground with other living creatures, the chicken as well as the lion. Our essential common ground is blood: everything in the animal kingdom has blood. Throughout

Scripture this touchpoint of common ground—blood—is used to teach about the value of life itself.

The first Passover. Just before the exodus, the Israelites were taught to take animal blood, specifically lamb's blood, and put it on their door frames. This was the blood of the Passover lamb. "When I see the blood, I will pass over you, and no plague will befall you to destroy you, when I strike the land of Egypt" (Exodus 12:13). The Israelites did as God instructed. The lifeblood of the lamb was of great value. It saved their lives.

The sacrificial system. After the exodus, God gave Israel further instructions about the blood of animals. Blood was to be handled with care and respect, as if it were precious. God did this to teach something of great value in the history of redemption. The key passage is in Leviticus 17: "Any one ... who takes in hunting any beast or bird that may be eaten shall pour out its blood and cover it with earth. For the life of every creature is its blood: its blood is its life" (13-14). God thus inculcates into the people of Israel a respect for life. Blood equals life. Have a high regard for blood, God tells the people, even if it is just the blood of a game bird.

Notice again the verbal yellow highlight. What God says with emphasis, he says *twice*: "For the life of every creature is its blood: its blood is its life." Human life is treasured above all else in creation, yet it holds in common with all other living animals the treasure of life itself. This common ground is blood. It represents the gift of life.

Blood is inseparable from redemption. I suppose God could have chosen anything to symbolize life. But he chose blood for a profound reason. He pointed to the reason earlier, when he taught Israel to put the blood of the lamb on their doorposts. Now he states the reason plainly: blood is to be handled with extreme care because it stands not only for life itself, but also for redemption of life. "And I have given it for you on the altar to make atonement for your souls, for it is the blood that makes atonement by the life" (Leviticus 17:11).

Blood is used to symbolize the covering over of our sins before a holy God, lest we die. This covering over is serious business. It can't happen apart from death; the shedding of blood. The story God tells throughout Scripture is that one death must happen so that another can be prevented. That is the way of the Passover, the way of the Mosaic law, and the way of the cross.

Is there anything more valuable than human life and the redemption of human life? By virtue of our salvation, Christians have inherited from God a profound commitment to the sanctity of life and a devotion to make Christ known. Both come from holding blood (life) precious.

Intrinsically Sacred

When I was 10 years old, a boy my age died right before my eyes. We were running down a sidewalk when he collapsed and died from heart failure. There was no blood spilled, but there was death. Forty-six years later I know the very spot, the single square of concrete upon which he fell. I could walk you right to it and point it out to you. That spot is sacred to me because on that spot life was lost, human life, a sharer in that common grace called the brotherhood of man.

A few years ago I visited Dachau, the former Nazi concentration camp outside of Munich. My two sons were with me. We walked through the various buildings and among the foundations of dismantled barracks. "Here," we were told, "is the place where Christian pastors, arrested for defending Jews, were all kept together so they could not infect the other prisoners with their teaching." A little further, "Here is where medical experiments were conducted on Jews until they died." Again, "There are the hooks from which people were hung." I could not speak. When I tried, only a whisper came out.

Whether in the natural death of one boy or the demonic devouring of millions, life and death should have an arresting claim upon us. As creatures who share in life and who will share in death, we should delight in life and grieve over death with a tender reverence. Life and death are sacred because human life is precious. That is the lesson of the simple ceremony commanded in Leviticus 17.

This injection of the sacred—this endowment concerning the preciousness of human life—starts with the Passover and continues with the sacrificial system. It starts with animals and birds given for food. The blood of an animal sacrificed on your behalf secures your own life. Certain good manners must attend even the preparation: "Pour out its blood and cover it with earth" (Leviticus 17:23). Never drink it; it is not common water. Blood is the gift of life, which is the gift of God.

Get out your yellow highlighter. God is speaking with emphasis.

The Rule of Repetition

Saying things twice or with emphasis is part of the rule of repetition, or over-communication: what we consider most important we repeat. As a father, I over-communicate often: there are certain things my children heard from me every day. One year, my daughter actually made a list of "Things Papa Says" for a framed Christmas present. They were mostly bits of silliness meant to entertain, but our children heard plenty and often the things I consider essential for their well-being. Every loving parent repeats the essentials. This drives teenagers crazy — so be it. The choices they make in the hour of temptation will set the course of their lives in one direction or another. So we repeat ourselves.

God does the same. Preeminent concerns are taught through repetition. "Verily, verily" or "Truly, truly" was the idiomatic way Jesus used a verbal yellow highlighter. Paul wrote, "Finally, then, brothers, we ask and urge you in the Lord Jesus, that as you received from us how you ought to live and to please God, just as you are doing, that you do so more and more" (1 Thessalonians 4:1). In context, Paul is about to call them to lives of sexual integrity: "For this is the will of God, your sanctification: that you abstain from sexual immorality" (4:3). This plea is not new: Paul had taught it to them in person. So here he writes *again* what he knows they had already *received*. Paul even acknowledges that they are already *practicing* this lifestyle ("just as you are doing"), yet he tells them again because of its significance.

Furthermore, Paul is "asking *and* urging" (note the repetition). So important is this matter to their faith that he adds a warning to it, that "whoever disregards this, disregards not man but God, who gives his Holy Spirit to you" (4:8). And even this warning is a repetition of something Paul says "we told you *beforehand* and solemnly warned you" (4:6).

Paul is saying: I don't know how I could possibly put this more strongly.

Now consider the mind-boggling repetition that God establishes for the Israelites in Leviticus 17 concerning lifeblood during the time they were in the wilderness. The immediate context is hunger and the processing of meat— specifically livestock raised for food (sheep, oxen, goats) and wild game such as deer. But the context is also worship.

This happens after the people had been delivered (redeemed) out of their bondage to Egypt and before the time of Solomon when a permanent temple would be built. During this time, a mobile temple was set up to serve as the central focus of the community. God dwelt ("tabernacled") there by his Spirit, so it was also called the tent of meeting, because that is where you could go and meet with God.

In Leviticus 17, God tells the people that when they are ready to eat meat, they should bring their livestock to the tent of meeting and butcher it there. But because the context is also giving thanks to God, it is more accurate to say they should *sacrifice* the animals there: "bring them to the LORD, to the priest at the entrance of the tent of meeting, and *sacrifice* them as sacrifices of peace offerings to the LORD" (17:5).

The priest would then ensure the blood was properly drained and capture some to throw it on the altar. "And the priest shall throw the blood on the altar of the LORD at the entrance of the tent of meeting and burn the fat for a pleasing aroma to the LORD" (17:6). The family, we may conclude, would then enjoy the meat with a thankful heart.

Every person, family, clan, and tribe received this reminder of the preciousness of blood as often as they desired chicken soup or lamb chops. Every day, hundreds or thousands of times, the priests slaughtered countless animals. Year-in and year-out, every family of all the tribes received this central lesson again and again: "This shall be a statute forever for them throughout their generations" (17:7).

The lesson repeated ad infinitum was that blood is life! God told them, "You live by your blood. You will be redeemed by the blood of the lamb. Keep faith and you will see how this is so." The message never stopped. "Your blood—your life—is precious to me. But your sins separate us. By the shedding of blood I shall cover your sins." These lessons were taught together, as they are today whenever we eat and give thanks for our food—worship and the preservation of life brought together into a single event. God wants us to know that the sacrificial shedding of blood and the preservation of life can never be separated. Like some conjoined twins, they live off the same heart.

Earth Is Not a Safe Place to Live

When Jesus said, "You are of more value than many sparrows" (Matthew 10:31), it was not to build up your self-esteem. It was to make you live more courageously in this sin-sick, wicked world. He actually said, "Fear not! You are of more value than many sparrows."

Despite the endless repeated call of God to hold each life precious, powerful dark forces constantly rise up to treat the less powerful as mere sparrows. Jesus wants his people to look squarely at the harshness of the world and know that there are times when "Brother will deliver brother over to death, and the father his child, and children will rise against parents and have them put to death, and you will be hated by all for my name's sake" (Matthew 10:21-22). Earth is not a safe place to live: "woe to you, O earth and sea, for the devil has come down to you in great wrath" (Revelation 12:12).

There are times when courage will be required of our faith. When we are in the crosshairs of destruction, we will need the courage that comes from trusting that God holds our lives dearly.

> And do not fear those who kill the body but cannot kill the soul. Rather fear him who can destroy both soul and body in hell. Are not two sparrows sold for a penny? And not one of them will fall to the ground apart from your Father. But even the hairs of your head are all numbered. Fear not, therefore; you are of more value than many sparrows. (Matthew 10:28-31)

When we see the lives of others being devoured, we will need the courage of our faith if we are to react like Job and testify, "I broke the fangs of the unrighteous and made him drop his prey from his teeth" (Job 29:17). Jesus is saying, "Be courageous! Hold each life precious." For "precious is their blood in his sight" (Psalm 72:14).

TWO
BLOOD-GUILT

God's Response to the Shedding of Innocent Blood

Sing praises to the Lord, who sits enthroned in Zion!
Tell among the peoples his deeds!
For he who avenges blood is mindful of them;
he does not forget the cry of the afflicted. — *Psalm 9:11-12*

Why should I save his hide?
Why should I right this wrong
When I have come so far
And struggled for so long?
If I speak, I am condemned.
If I stay silent, I am damned! — *Jean Valjean, Les Misérables* [5]

Between 1882 and 1968, nearly 3,500 Black
Americans were lynched in the United States. Among
them were Thomas Shipp and Abram Smith, two men
murdered in Marion, Indiana, on August 7, 1930. The
night before, they had been arrested and charged with
the armed robbery and murder of a white man, and the
rape of a white woman. The case was never solved,[6] partly
because, with thousands in attendance, the men were hung
from a tree in the town center on the night of their arrest.

Lawrence Beitler/Bettmann/Corbis

What is God's response to the lynching of Thomas Shipp and Abram Smith? Who shall be held accountable for their lifeblood? Surely the handful of men who actually did the hanging. Yes, of course. If I tell you that they were stoned and beaten to death before being strung up, then you will agree that all those who picked up a stone, or hit these men with a rake handle, or simply stood by cheering on the aggressors—these all share in the bloodguilt.

Studio photographer Lawrence Beitler captured the scene. His photo of a crowd gathered around the tree from which the two men hung is the iconic picture of lynching in America. At first I thought it was good that he captured the horrible truth, no matter how graphic and anguishing. It arouses a righteous anger that ought to lead to righteous action. Then I learned that photos like this were routinely turned into postcards and sent to friends.

Beitler himself made and sold thousands of copies of this picture in the days that followed, profiting from the shedding of innocent blood.[7] He treated it as a spectacle no different than photographing the Kentucky Derby. What is God's response to these actions?

And what about the thousands who did not actively kill these two men but watched it happen? What guilt do they bear? What about those who bought the photographs? What of those who received them and tacked them to their iceboxes? What guilt does the citizenry at-large bear? Many who were not in attendance that night may have soon thereafter attended church or had dinner or engaged in commerce with those who stood under that tree and watched approvingly until the bodies slowly stopped swinging. What guilt would I bear if I had been a pastor or elder in this town?

To answer these questions we need to ask another: what does the Bible say about bloodguilt, the wrath of God, and the courage required of our faith?

Bloodguilt

"Bloodguilt" is a blunt, almost vulgar term. It hits rudely, like a slap in the face. It is God's chosen term to arouse godly fear and compel decisive action.[8] It is a word of awakening, forcing us to recognize an unbreakable linkage: God's image is debased and his wrath justly incited every time a person made in God's image is unjustly destroyed. There is no debasing of God's image without consequences.

Bloodguilt requires God's vengeance and vindication. It stands as an indictment against the sin of shedding innocent blood, but it is also a promise, of sorts, to victims. These are they who cried out to God and received no immediate answer. To them, it may have seemed either that God did not care or was powerless to intervene. Psalm 9:11-12 reminds us that neither of these options is true—this is a false choice: "Sing praises to the Lord, who sits enthroned in Zion! Tell among the peoples his deeds! *For he who avenges blood is mindful of them; he does not forget the cry of the afflicted.*"

What do the afflicted cry out to God?

- In Psalm 31:2, they cry, "*Incline* your ear to me; *rescue* me speedily!"
- In Psalm 35:23, they cry, "*Awake* and *rouse* yourself for my *vindication*, for my cause, my God and my Lord!"
- In Psalm 54:1, they cry, "O God, *save* me by your name, and *vindicate* me by your might."
- In Psalm 59:1, they cry, "*Deliver* me from my enemies, O my God; *protect* me from those who rise up against me."
- In Psalm 59:2, they cry, "*deliver* me from those who work evil, and *save* me from bloodthirsty men."
- In Psalm 70:5, they cry, "I am poor and needy; *hasten* to me, O God! You are my help and my *deliverer*; O Lord, do not delay!"
- In Psalm 71:4 they cry, "*Rescue* me, O my God, from the hand of the wicked, from the grasp of the unjust and cruel man."
- In Psalm 109:21, they cry, "But you, O God my Lord, *deal* on my behalf for your name's sake."
- In Psalm 140:1, they cry, "*Preserve* me from violent men."

Each of these Psalms involves the threat of bloodshed against the innocent. God does not forget such cries: he remains *mindful* of them and regards any innocent blood shed with oppression as *bloodguilt*. God does not slough off suffering. And while he has his own reasons for delaying avenging wrath, he will not pardon it—he still has ample time to repay, and there is no statute of limitations. Even if you are the king of Judah, as was Jehoiakim, there is a blood-reckoning for bloodguilt, for Jehoiakim "filled Jerusalem with innocent blood, and the Lord would *not* pardon" (2 Kings 24:4).

God Protects What He Loves

Many regard God as capricious, pouring out his wrath for what seem like minor infractions of rules that are difficult to understand, but what we see in Scripture is a consistent and compassionate God whose righteous anger vindicates those who suffer injustice. To do anything less would, in fact, be unloving and immoral. God loves those made in his image with a fierce and jealous love, and he protects what he loves with all his power.

Justice derives from love. When God avenges and vindicates, he is simply demonstrating his own love. What you hold as valuable you expect to be respected by others, because you think those valued things have a *right* to be honored. When we talk about *human rights*, we mean that there is an inherent dignity of personhood, that those created as image-bearers of God have an inherent right not only to exist but to be treated justly, completely apart from matters of wealth or talent or pedigree.

But history demonstrates that the concept of human rights is not always acknowledged. "A righteous man knows the *rights* of the poor; a wicked man does not understand such knowledge" (Proverbs 29:7). That verse summarizes much of human conflict. Some of us fear God and acknowledge the rights of others made in his image; others do not fear God and so treat people as unworthy of respect.

If you hear an intruder breaking into your home you immediately call 911. You *expect* the police to come quickly to your defense. If your cries are not answered in time, you turn to the courts for justice. When the "justice" system works as it is designed to do, the harm you suffered determines the punishment: the greater the harm, the greater the punishment that is meted out. Justice demands it. Love requires it.

Love is moral in nature. If this is still hard to grasp, consider this: If I come across a man raping a woman, I cannot love them both in the same way: in that circumstance, love to the woman will look like rescue while love to the man may look like violence. This is because love is inherently *moral* in character.

Suppose I approach the terrorized woman and her brutal assailant and say, "I love you both equally and must express that love in the same fashion. God does not want you to violate this woman, but please do not think he is angry: because God is love, he does not get angry. Isn't that amazing!"[9]

The woman would denounce my faith as cowardly, irrational, and evil. So would you. Love must love righteousness and hate evil. Love must be passionately committed to right over wrong. It must pick sides. It must fight for the weak and the innocent and oppose the violent and the wicked. Therefore, I must scream my lungs out, push the man off of her, shout for a neighbor to call the police — do *something*. If the rapist turns on me with his knife and I lose my life in the process of defending the woman, what will they say? There is no greater love than to risk your life for another (cf. John 15:13).

This is the sense in which I can read the disturbing, unsheathed words of Psalm 5:4-6, and see them as consistent with the God of infinite love: "You are not a God who delights in wickedness; evil may not dwell with you. The boastful shall not stand before your eyes; you hate all evildoers. You destroy those who speak lies; the LORD abhors the bloodthirsty and deceitful man."

When the wicked devour the innocent, at that moment and in that context, God chooses sides: his love demands it. In that sense, the psalmist says, God loves the one and abhors the other.

God Protects Human Life by the Principle of Justice

As Noah stepped from the ark, he was blessed with the same life-affirming commission Adam had received: "Be fruitful and multiply and fill the earth" (Genesis 9:1). The difference this time was that the law of sin and death were now at work in all mankind. The essential command from God was the same, merely adapted to a world now fallen. Therefore, to restrain evil and promote the public welfare, God added:

> The fear of you and the dread of you shall be upon
> every beast of the earth and upon every bird of the
> heavens, upon everything that creeps on the ground
> and all the fish of the sea. Into your hand they are
> delivered. Every moving thing that lives shall be food
> for you. And as I gave you the green plants, I give you
> everything. But you shall not eat flesh with its life,
> that is, its blood. (Genesis 9:1-4)

Sin has changed the nature of things. Before the fall,
animals were under our dominion, and they still are, but
now they live in dread and fear of us. For the first time God
explicitly adds meat to what we may freely eat. But notice
the regulations. From the first moment we are given the
right to eat meat, we are forbidden to eat the flesh of any
animal while it is still alive—that is, while its lifeblood is
coursing through it. The reasons are the same as we saw in
Leviticus 17 (and Deuteronomy 12). Blood represents life,
and life is holy. We show reverence for life by treating even
the blood of animals as separate, or holy, unto God.

Then, in his directives to Noah, God pivots from
the blood of animals to the blood of our fellow man: "for
your lifeblood I will require a reckoning; from every beast
I will require it and from man" (Genesis 9:5).

I am not sure what this law means in reference to
the animals. I suspect that it at least means that when an
animal kills a man, God avenges it by having the animal
destroyed (cf. Exodus 21:28-29). The animal has crossed
a line. A bear that attacks and kills a human being in Yel-
lowstone Park is taken down. It has both lost its natural

fear and become aggressive in a way that presents an ongoing danger to human life. As a result, its life is forfeit.

Then comes the larger principle, the principle of reckoning or retributive justice. "Whoever sheds the blood of man, by man shall his blood be shed, for God made man in his own image" (Genesis 9:6).

Pull out your yellow highlighter. God has spoken something holy and fearful.

The Just Wages of Bloodguilt

You might ask, "If it is wrong for man to take human life, how is it right that God says, 'Whoever sheds the blood of man, *by man* shall his blood be shed'?" Doesn't this permit the very thing it outlaws?

I answer in two ways. First, the principle of justice reflects God's commitment to his own moral excellence. The just penalty for taking human life is the forfeiture of human life. The wages of bloodguilt is death. At the same time, God is foreshadowing his intent to bind this principle of justice onto those commissioned to restrain evil in the community as judges and other lawful authorities. [10]

The principle is expanded upon in Leviticus:

Whoever takes a human life shall surely be put to death. Whoever takes an animal's life shall make it good, life for life. If anyone injures his neighbor, as he has done it shall be done to him, fracture for fracture, eye for eye, tooth for tooth; whatever injury he has given a person shall be given to him. (24:17-20)

Such words have been used to justify heinous acts of revenge. Yet what they point to properly is God extending a measure of his own sovereign authority to civil or governmental authorities (Romans 13:1). They are a gift of God for the purpose of protecting life and promoting the common good in a community affected by sin (Romans 13:4).

God Protects Human Life through Natural Law

All people of every culture, of every religion or none, throughout all the ages, know that shedding innocent blood is evil. It is hard-wired into our consciences. The most committed postmodernist who believes that truth is relative and that we must individually decide for ourselves what is right or wrong will object vehemently if I bind him, take his wallet, and pace back and forth with a gun wondering if I should leave any witnesses. He will not say, "Whatever you think is right for you is right." He will immediately and vigorously seek to impose his morality on me. He will ask me to do what is right for him.

Cain killed Abel long before God gave us the Ten Commandments. Nonetheless, God called Cain to accountability, asking Cain where his brother was. This was an indictment, not an inquiry. Cain in turn, attempted to hide his crime by responding with a deflecting answer, "I do not know; am I my brother's keeper?" (Genesis 4:9). He knew he had done evil, yet tried to hide it.

Cain's response is instructive. It reveals his understanding that the instinctive, hardwired, natural-law command not to kill his brother also required him to act protectively toward his brother. It is not just "do him no harm," but also "bless him and look out for him." So Cain tried to hide his violation of the natural law against murder in a strange way—by shirking his ethical obligation to protect his brother's life. If he could void the weaker component of this instinctive law, he assumed he could void the stronger component as well. "Am I my brother's keeper?" The answer is yes. Abel's lifeblood was a treasure to God and deserved Cain's protection.

God Protects Human Life through the Sixth Commandment

Because our consciences are corrupted by sin and can even become so corrupt as to basically be non-functioning, God reveals his holy character and the moral demands that flow from it. "Be holy, for I am holy" (Leviticus 11:45), he says, and then the sixth commandment reads, "You shall not murder" (Exodus 20:13). What we must not do is explicit; what we must do is implied. What is implied in the call not to take life is the call to keep life or preserve life, as Cain recognized. So we read,

> When an ox gores a man or a woman to death, the ox shall be stoned, and its flesh shall not be eaten, but the owner of the ox shall not be liable. But if the ox has been accustomed to gore in the past, and its owner has been warned but has not kept it in, and it kills a man or a woman, the ox shall be stoned and its owner also shall be put to death. (Exodus 21:28-29)

Manslaughter is the unintentional or accidental *taking* of human life. *Negligent homicide* is the *failure to act positively to protect* human life when there is a clear responsibility and opportunity to do so. Failure to protect and preserve human life when it is in our power is a violation of the sixth commandment. It is not enough to say, "I didn't do it" if you could have tried to prevent it. You really are your brother's keeper, and for this there is a blood-reckoning.

Again we read, "When you build a new house, you shall make a parapet for your roof, that you may not bring the guilt of blood upon your house, if anyone should fall from it" (Deuteronomy 22:8). In this case, we are to think ahead and watch out to keep our neighbor safe.

All these are positive applications of the command, "You shall not murder." We are morally bound to think and act in ways that protect and preserve human life. Another way to say this is simply, "love your neighbor."

God Protects Human Life by His Great Command

Whenever Jesus pointed to the central command of the Old Testament, he always joined to it a second point of emphasis.

And one of the scribes…asked him, "Which commandment is the most important of all?" Jesus answered, "The most important is, 'Hear, O Israel: The Lord our God, the Lord is one. And you shall love the Lord your God with all your heart and with all your soul and with all your mind and with all your strength.' The second is this: "You shall love your

neighbor as yourself." There is no other commandment greater than these. (Mark 12:28-34) [11]

Inextricably linked to the Great Commandment,
therefore, is "love your neighbor as yourself" (Leviticus
19:18). The apostle Paul enlarges the point,

> For the commandments, "You shall not commit
> adultery, You shall not murder, You shall not steal,
> You shall not covet," and any other commandment,
> are summed up in this word: "You shall love your
> neighbor as yourself." Love does no wrong to a
> neighbor; therefore love is the fulfilling of the law.
> (Romans 13:9-10)

In other words, we fulfill the actual obligations of the
sixth commandment by earnestly heeding this corollary
of the Great Commandment.

Consider again that photo of the lynching of Thomas
Shipp and Abram Smith, with all those people gathered
in Marion's town square. This commandment to "love
your neighbor as yourself" explains the discomfort I
feel in looking at the photo. I see the evil of those who
murdered these men, but I see the larger lack of love. The
photo is proof positive that much of the city was stained
with blood. The law of love demands far more than
not shedding innocent blood: it demands that we act to
preserve life. Passive acceptance is damnable.

The character of Jean Valjean in the musical *Les
Misérables* is tested on this point. An innocent man is

about to be punished, and Jean Valjean has the power to stop it, but only by confessing that he is the wanted man. He wrestles with the demands of God: "Why should I save his hide? Why should I right this wrong, when I have come so far, and struggled for so long? If I speak, I am condemned. If I stay silent, I am damned!"

Training for the Day of Our Own Testing

In Deuteronomy 21, God instructs his people explicitly about the negative and positive ethical demands of love. He is training them to know the will of God concerning the shedding of innocent blood: "If in the land that the Lord your God is giving you to possess someone is found slain, lying in the open country, and it is not known who killed him, then your elders and your judges shall come out, and they shall measure the distance to the surrounding cities" (1-2).

If your loved one is murdered, you stop everything. You close up your shop, you gather your friends and family, you weep and groan before a Sovereign God. You plan a funeral and consult with law enforcement. You may mark the spot with a plaque or flowers, or at least mark the place of burial. You will walk with a sorrow that will never go away. For the rest of your life, faith in God will mean, in large part, trusting him with this unspeakable heartache (2 Corinthians 1:4) and believing him when he says he will avenge and vindicate (2 Corinthians 1:9).

None of this happens when a stranger is murdered. We go to work, do a load of laundry, cook dinner, play with our kids, mow the lawn, bless God, and go to bed. But God grieves the loss. To him it is personal. In addition, he knows that if we do not feel the loss in some way, we become less feeling. We make peace with death and become hardened to the laws of love. Therefore, when a stranger is murdered, our leaders should make sure that the whole community thinks through the death of the unknown man from God's perspective and comes to feel something of the loss that God feels.

It begins with establishing jurisdiction. The closer we are to the body, the more responsible we are. Again, this is a hardwired law of the human conscience. In the parable of the Good Samaritan, Jesus points out that the priest and the Levite "passed by on the other side" (Luke 10:32). In an effort to reduce their sense of personal responsibility, they got as much distance from the man left for dead as possible.

In Deuteronomy 21, however, the victim has died and the town nearest to the body must accept responsibility for it. Accordingly, the whole town is summoned to halt business as usual. The leaders are called to lead the entire community through a time-consuming and expensive ritual *designed to help them all feel something of the loss God feels*:

> And the elders of the city that is nearest to the slain man shall take a heifer that has never been worked and that has not pulled in a yoke. And the elders of that city shall bring the heifer down to a valley with running water, which is neither plowed nor sown, and shall break the heifer's neck there in the valley. Then the priests, the sons of Levi, shall come forward, for

the Lord your God has chosen them to minister to him and to bless in the name of the Lord, and by their word every dispute and every assault shall be settled. And all the elders of that city nearest to the slain man shall wash their hands over the heifer whose neck was broken in the valley. (Deuteronomy 21:3-7)

A prized piece of good commercial livestock is sacrificed. Good land, marked by flowing water, is now a memorial plot. The people feel through economic loss something of the emotional loss that God feels. Then the leaders must testify. They pray for all to hear the essential lesson at the heart of this matter: "Our hands did not shed this blood, nor did our eyes see it shed" (21:7).

Notice that they needed to testify to two things. They needed to testify that they did not *actively* take life and they needed to testify that they did not *passively* watch it happen. The law being reinforced again is this: do not shed innocent blood *and* do not let others shed innocent blood without a fight. Failure to do either leads to bloodguilt and judgment.

But notice further that even though the people could testify before God that they did not shed this blood or passively accept another doing so, they were *still* stained with bloodguilt. Through this ritual—in which everyone is essentially called to renew their vows to both the negative and positive demands of brotherly love—they ask God to remove real guilt. By shedding the blood of the heifer they pray for God to find his own way to cover over their bloodguilt with sacrificed blood. They seek atonement for this sin: "Accept *atonement*, O Lord, for your people Israel, whom you have redeemed, and do not set the guilt of innocent blood in the midst of your people Israel, so that their blood guilt be atoned for" (21:8).

How we respond to the shedding of innocent blood is vital. The day we stop nurturing respect for human life is the day we begin diminishing the value of human life. The day we stop reminding ourselves of the preeminent value of human life is the day we begin submitting to the priorities of this sinful world. Where we are not fighting for life, we are making peace with death. Where we are not pained by the death of the innocent, we are growing hard-hearted to the holy will of God. Feel the pain and prepare for the fight!

"So you shall *purge* the guilt of innocent blood from your midst, when you do what is right in the sight of the Lord" (21:9).

Doing Right in the Sight of the Lord

We can look now on those who stood then in Marion, Indiana, and see the moral fog.

Those people were shrouded in self-preserving cowardice and passive acceptance of injustice. A relatively small number were outright murderers. Many others, while not actively aggressive, nevertheless tacitly approved of the violence through their passivity. Not acting was itself an action; deciding not to take sides was to side with the murderers.

To apply today's terminology to that August night in 1930, many of the bystanders, being against murder in principle, would have considered themselves "personally pro-life." But none present during the murders, from those who hurled stones to those who were personally but passively "pro-life," *did what was right in the sight of the Lord*. As a result, together they are stained with bloodguilt. Without atonement, they face the avenging and vindicating wrath of God.

Being personally pro-life but otherwise passive is a cowardly and shameful position. Christ is trying to show this in the way he describes the behavior of the priest and the Levite in his parable (Luke 10:25-37). Seeing a man beaten and about to die, they let it stand unchallenged. They might well comfort themselves, "That is just horrible. I do not believe in that." However, merely *believing* that murder is wrong does not qualify as obedience to the commandments of God we have been discussing in this chapter. When you can live with death, work around it, or let it go unchallenged, you are not pro-life.

Samaritan compassion. Doing right in the sight of the Lord means acting to stop the shedding of innocent blood. The only person in Jesus' parable who is pro-life according to the demands of love is the Samaritan. Only he was willing to make the nearly dead man's problem his own. Only he was willing to see the victim's suffering as his own. Only he was willing to act according to what *he* would cry out for if their positions had been reversed. This is the meaning of compassion—literally, to *suffer with* the object of one's love. So the Samaritan picked up the injured man, bandaged his wounds, took him to the inn, paid for his care, and promised to return and pay more if needed. This is Christianity in action.

Pilate was also personally pro-life—you realize that, don't you? He was unwilling to shed innocent blood *personally*. But he was also unwilling to stop it. Doing right in the eyes of the Lord means, first, not shedding innocent blood. But second, it means *taking action to prevent it from happening*. Pilate understood the negative demand of love, but he sought to escape the positive demand. "He took water and washed his hands before the crowd, saying, 'I am innocent of this man's blood; see to it yourselves' (Matthew 27:24). According to Deuteronomy 21, Pilate's hand-washing was an exercise in self-deception. Far from establishing his innocence, it sealed his guilt. Bemoaning the murder of the innocent is not enough. Rescuing the innocent is required: "*Rescue* the weak and the needy; *deliver* them from the hand of the wicked" (Psalm 82:4). "*Rescue* those who are being taken away to death; *hold back* those who are stumbling to the slaughter" (Proverbs 24:11).

Courage Is Required of Our Faith

Now Photoshop yourself into the picture of the crowd in Marion that night and we come to the heart of the matter. What would you have done—assuming you were Caucasian and therefore felt safe simply to be present? Would you have joined in beating Thomas Shipp and Abram Smith to death? Would you have assisted in the lynching? Perhaps not.

Would you have watched? Possibly. Maybe you would have just gone home so that you did not *have* to watch. That way you could pretend you didn't actually know what was happening. I fear that might have been my strategy.

Clearly, if we are to do what is right in the eyes of the Lord then we must, when faced with the imminent death of the innocent, fear God more than man and let our faith in him quicken into courage.

An exercise in speculation. So there you are in Marion, Indiana, that night in 1930. Speak up, and you risk at least a scalding rebuke from family and friends. What if you are a store clerk and your boss is in the crowd? Speak up and you may lose your job. What if you are a powerful business leader? Speak up and you will lose customers, plus all those pats on the back from people who honor you for your business acumen and public charity. What if you are a Christian leader? Now you are Jean Valjean. Speak up and you will lose all you have worked for, but stay silent and you are damned.

What if, on the following Sunday, your pastor says to you after church, "This lynching business is a political issue and I am about preaching the gospel" — do you have the moral clarity and courage to do what is right in the sight of the Lord? Do you have the courage to say, respectfully but firmly, "No, pastor, I'm sorry, but this is far more than a political issue. You are not preaching the gospel when you assent to evil. In fact, now you are using God to disobey God." Do you have that clarity, that courage?

Or maybe your pastor says, "I know there are people in this church who feel guilty about their involvement in the lynching. I do not want to make them feel worse." Do you have the courage to say, "I am afraid, pastor, that perhaps it is *you* who does not want to feel worse. Leaving people in guilt is not your calling. Even an unbeliever can do that."

No speculation needed. We do not have to speculate about how we might have responded if we were living in Marion, Indiana, in 1930. We do not need to speculate about what we would do if we were in Pilate's shoes long ago. We do not need to guess if we would have risked our lives or not for the children fleeing to Le Chambon, France. We only have to ask ourselves how we are responding to the shedding of innocent blood as it is happening now, in our own town.

Abortion, like lynching, is the shedding of innocent blood, is it not? Have you made peace with it? Have you navigated around it? Can you lift up your hands and say, "I did not shed this blood, nor did I see it happening"?

Or have you found a way to feel the loss of these unknown innocents, even if it is only some sort of economic loss? The fact that over 6,000 pregnancy-help centers and maternity homes have been established—all by charity in just the last forty years since abortion was legalized in most countries—suggests that many Christians have decided not to make peace with death. They have set up ministries in good commercial property to stop it. They have paid for rent and staff and ultrasound machines in order to help mothers and their babies escape the agony and violence of abortion. It is noble, it is honorable, and it is nothing less than the Underground Railroad of this generation.

Have you understood with moral clarity the need to rescue the weak and the innocent? Have you asked God for the moral courage to do so? When I asked myself these questions a while back, I came up short. I was Pilate. My silence had left my own congregation with bloodguilt. This is all the more tragic because in the unfolding glory of the redemption, God has gone so much farther than to offer the blood of a heifer.

I decided to repent.

Fetus aborted 8 weeks after conception.

THREE
BLOOD-ATONEMENT

Christ's Provision for the Shedding of Innocent Blood

You have come ... to Jesus, the mediator of a new covenant, and to the sprinkled blood that speaks a better word than the blood of Abel. — Hebrews 12:22-24

Whatever difficulties there appear in your way, whatever doubts arise in your heart, from your sins and guilt, whatever objections your fears may put forth, there is the blood of the Lamb, that will answer all. — Richard Alleine (1611-1681)

If we are to meet the enemy of souls on the battle-ground of bloodguilt, squirrel-hunting shotguns will not do. We need armor-piercing bullets. I learned this one day when I met a man who flared his eyes at me, pointed his finger, and said, "God can never forgive me. I killed my wife."

I realized then that some experiences mark people in specific ways. This is especially true when it comes to the shedding of innocent blood. People who recognize their guilt in this area have trouble engaging in any discussion of the gospel that fails to explicitly and specifically address their experience, no matter how accurate it may be otherwise. General gospel assurances about God's love will not help because bloodguilt speaks with specificity. It provides memories of exact times and places, to which certain sounds and smells can all bear witness.

This man was impaled on the justice of a loving God. He knew instinctively that the just wages of his sin *must* be death (Romans 6:23), so he needed to know how the gospel could deal with his bloodguilt. His pointed finger said, "I don't think it can happen."

Bloodguilt vs. Blood-Atonement

We often say in our home, "The devil always beats his own," and here was proof: this man was clearly tormented. Seeing his dire situation and realizing he was well-armed to fend off any good news, I pivoted from the general question, "Can God forgive us our sins?" to the specific, "Can God forgive a man for killing his wife?"

Our conversation was lively, and not nearly as tidy and orderly as I will retell it here for the sake of clarity. But the recounting does reflect my earnest attempt to explain the gospel as blood for blood—blood-atonement capable of cleansing away his very real bloodguilt.

I began with, "I agree with you. God undoubtedly loved your wife, and it would take a miracle for him to forgive you."

I wanted him to see that God agrees with his conscience. God treasured his wife's lifeblood and would surely avenge it. He would vindicate her worth. There is hell to pay.

The man was not prepared to be agreed with. Then I offered him proof. "If you have any doubt about it, consider the cross of Christ. On the cross, Christ was 'wounded for our transgressions; he was crushed for our iniquities' (Isaiah 53:5)."

I told him, "On the cross, God calculated the just penalty that you should pay for killing your wife. Then he executed that punishment in full on his own son. It was life for life, blood for blood. The more horrific your sin and the more damnable you see that it truly was, then the more you can understand how much Christ truly suffered on the cross in your stead."

Of course, when you talk about the cross as God's wrath and judgment upon bloodguilt, the kindness of God also peeks through.

I continued, "If you take the death of Christ *for* your own, then God says he will honor the death of Christ *as* your own. If you trust in Christ for the forgiveness of your sins, then God would be *justified* to forgive you and cleanse you from all your sins. This includes the sins you discount but that God does not. And it includes the sins that appear insurmountable, like killing your wife."

"How is this possible? When you accept the death of Christ as your own—as full punishment paid for the full punishment due—there is nothing left to be punished. It has all been purged away. God is 'just to forgive us and cleanse us from all unrighteousness (1 John 1:9)."

"The same unbreakable and inflexible principle of justice that condemns you right now defends you going forward. God will always do right and act justly. If he punished you *in Christ* for your bloodguilt, it would be wrong to punish you again for the same sins. If you put your faith in Christ and in the cross, God is justified to show you mercy, even for killing your wife."

Thus began a hearing of the gospel that confirmed the woeful truth of his life and yet came across as the profound good news that it is. "For the wages of sin is death, but the free gift of God is eternal life in Christ Jesus our Lord" (Romans 6:23).[12]

Abortion vs. the Forgiveness of God

We do not meet many people on the street marked by the bloodguilt of wife-killing. But every day we do interact with people marked by another specific kind of blood-guilt—abortion. Abortion is the defining experience of this generation. It is an experience involving the shedding of innocent blood, a sin of bloodguilt, a sin that can only be addressed by a forthright, compassionate, and unapologetic gospel. The living women (and men) damaged by their complicity in abortion need someone willing to bring the *main* thing—the cross—to bear on the *one* thing that most plagues their conscience and hamstrings their service to God.

Imagine preaching the gospel in the town of Dachau in the 1940s and intentionally avoiding, rather than addressing, how the death of Christ on the cross can atone (cover over and wash away) the murder of innocents. We are in much the same situation today.

Are we silent? If so, it may mean we are too cowardly or squeamish to say what must be said. Or it may mean that we ourselves don't believe that the death of Christ really can satisfy the demands of justice in the slaughter of innocents.

Or it may mean that we don't understand the nature of the cross well enough ourselves to see that it has the power to purge real bloodguilt. I'm referring to hard truths such as substitutionary punishment and blood atonement. These terms, along with bloodguilt, wrath, and judgment, are generally avoided today. Evidently, they are not seen as good connecting points with this generation. This is wrong, and exactly backwards. No other generation is more stained with bloodguilt than the current generation. No other word is more needed than one that can explain how bloodguilt can be removed.

The Scope of the Challenge

According to the Alan Guttmacher Institute, the research arm of Planned Parenthood, the world's largest abortion business, there are 42 million induced abortions worldwide every year.[13] This figure has held fairly constant for 30 years. In the US, a woman has to be at least 80 years of age not to have gone through some or all of her child-bearing years with abortion legal and accessible.

At current rates, one-third of all American women have had or will have at least one abortion by age 45.[14] The majority of American women have abortions to please a man or because they have been abandoned by a man. When you talk to someone today about the gospel, male or female, you are almost certainly talking to someone who has experienced abortion directly (the mother or father of an aborted child) or indirectly (related to or personally close to someone in that first category). That is, you are almost certainly talking to someone touched by personal bloodguilt and, whether they realize it or not, bearing the weight of that guilt.

According to Dr. David Reardon of the Elliot Institute, which specializes in researching the after-effects of abortion, "Women who make the choice to have an abortion subsequently face an elevated risk of death from all causes (especially suicide), more depression, more substance abuse, more delivery problems in later pregnancies, more divorces, more breast cancer . . . and the list goes on and on."[15]

If I visited a hospital full of wounded soldiers — some missing eyes, others arms, others bound to wheelchairs the rest of their lives — would you not expect me to say something about how the gospel offers everlasting life that includes new bodies raised up that can see and hear and leap for joy? If I am preaching Christ at a funeral, wouldn't it be strange to say nothing about the hope of the resurrection? If I am talking about the power of the gospel to the warring Hutu and Tutsi tribes in Rwanda, wouldn't you expect me to say something specific about the ability of the gospel to reconcile sworn enemies?

How is it possible to bring a liberating gospel to a generation that is so deeply and specifically marked by the bloodguilt of abortion and say nothing about it? Is it cowardice? Or is it that we have dulled all the guilt-removing edges off the gospel and now lack the precision and sharpness required to tackle real guilt?

Martin Luther is credited with saying,

> If I profess with the loudest voice and clearest exposition every portion of the truth of God except precisely that little point which the world and the devil are at that moment attacking, I am not confessing Christ, however boldly I may be professing Christ. Where the battle rages, there the loyalty of the soldier is proved, and to be steady on all the battle fronts besides is mere flight and disgrace if he flinches at that point. [16]

The times and the context determine what must be emphasized in the gospel. Our times are marked by the bloodguilt of abortion. It is the hallmark of our relativism and subjectivism. We define our own truth. We define our own morality. We define our own sexuality. We re-define personhood, marriage, and God himself in order to make things match up to our personal liking.

Abortion is central to this worldview. It is the practical glue that holds it together. You cannot "have sex" like you "have a hamburger" without some means of washing away the immediate consequences. Self-centered men especially covet legal abortion. Self-centered women see it as the very touchstone of their freedom and dignity. We even redefine the truth about abortion itself when the stark reality is that it is child-killing. It is child-sacrifice —

we kill one thing in order to get or keep something we want more. By sticking exclusively to the medical term "abortion" we sanitize these uncooperative facts to meet our needs and to keep guilt at bay.

The difficulty we are up against — the thing that renders so many of us passive and all but useless in this area — is that sexual sins and abortion do not play nice on this postmodern playground. To introduce them into the conversation as they really are at any meaningful level is simply too painful for us. So we often choose to offend God rather than man.

Policy and Pain

As I write this chapter, I am in China where a one-child policy forces abortion every day. The government boasts that this policy has eliminated over 400 million people, nearly 25 percent more than the entire US population. [17] Only they use a verbal sleight of hand and say that their policy has resulted in 400 million *fewer* people. Nearly everyone pretends it is no big deal. Yet Reggie Littlejohn reports,

> According to the World Health Organization, China has the highest female suicide rate of any country in the world, and it is the only nation in which more women than men kill themselves. Suicide is now the leading cause of death among rural Chinese women. Congressman Christopher Smith, who has taken a leading role in exposing the atrocities of the One-Child Policy through Congressional hearings

and other means, stated, "According to the most recent State Department Human Rights Report, one consequence of [China's] 'birth limitation policies' is that 56 percent of the world's female suicides occur in China, which is five times the world average, and approximately 500 suicides by women per day." [18]

Silence is not atonement. Silence covers up nothing. Only blood can atone for the shedding of innocent blood. The need for this message becomes evident the moment you break the silence.

I spoke in an unregistered church yesterday on 1 Thessalonians 4:3-6.

For this is the will of God, your sanctification: that you abstain from sexual immorality; that each one of you know how to control his own body in holiness and honor, not in the passion of lust like the Gentiles who do not know God; that no one transgress and wrong his brother in this matter, because the Lord is an avenger in all these things, as we told you before-hand and solemnly warned you.

I addressed the need to walk in sexual integrity and we talked about how we hurt one another when we fail in this area, especially when it leads to abortion. Some women stared quietly down. Men sat like figurines but with tears rolling down their cheeks. I simply noted that our sexual immorality and the abortions that come from it are painful and hurtful, and out came the pain.

We addressed abortion as bloodguilt and pointed to the cross as Christ shedding his innocent blood to pay for sin, including the sin of shedding innocent blood. This is where the battle rages. This is where the world and the devil have people by the neck. This is where we must aim without flinching.

To think of abortion as a secondary issue—or worse, a merely political issue—is to fundamentally misunderstand the defining experience of our times. It also means we fundamentally fail to see the central truth that the cross alone can cleanse the conscience from the debilitating effects of bloodguilt.

Our capacity to simply ignore the influence of abortion is crippling the effectiveness of the gospel. Abortion's role in the consciences of hundreds of millions of people in the United States alone is a boil that festers just under the surface of all Christian endeavors, and it needs lancing. It needs to be called out by name, confessed by name, and brought under a gospel that declares that there is no forgiveness for the shedding of innocent blood *except by the shedding of innocent blood*, that is, by the blood of Christ.

A Case Study in Cleansing the Conscience

When Nana brought her friend to see me at our local pregnancy help center, she sat silent for a while. Then she blurted out, "It hurts so much. But what can I do?"

Nana had come for help a week earlier. She was pregnant and here she found the help and courage she needed to parent or place for adoption. Now Nana brought her friend to see us.

"Please," she asked, "talk to my friend. She had an abortion and all she does is cry."

I said, "Some things truly are worth crying about."

Nana said, "I told her she could fast. I think that might help."

Both these women were nominal Muslims. I replied, "Fasting is a good thing. But in this case, I fear she could fast till she starved to death and never find any hope or assurance of forgiveness. No, I think she will need a miracle."

Then I made things worse. I took out some pictures of abortion and showed her why she felt so terrible. To be clear, I honestly did not do this to hurt her further. I did it to show her that she was right to be crying. I did it to show her that her tears were a sign that her conscience was working properly. She was not over-reacting.

Then I told her that I too was once convicted about my own guilt regarding the shedding of innocent blood. I never did anything to stop it. I allowed it to happen and did not care enough to even try to stop it. So I, too, was guilty.

She asked me what I did about it. I told her that I gave up all hope that there was anything I could do to remove the guilt. It was there and it was not going to go away by fasting or weeping. Trying to inflict some kind of punishment on myself could never pay it off. Trying to offset the guilt with good deeds never erases the blood-stain itself. No, I too needed a miracle.

Then I took my cue from Hebrews 12:24, which says that the blood of Christ "speaks a better word than the blood of Abel," or in her case, than the cries of her preborn child. I applied the cross of Christ to this one thing and explained it, saying, "There is no forgiveness for shedding innocent blood *except* by the shedding of innocent blood. Let me tell you about how Christ shed his innocent blood for all those who will accept it as a free gift of grace." When I finished, she whispered, "That is the most beautiful story I ever heard."

If the blood of a heifer, sacrificed in a field, pointed to the hope of atonement, as taught to us in Deuteronomy 21:1-10, how much more will the blood of Jesus, the true Lamb of God, cover over our bloodguilt? The cross spills blood for blood: *full payment made* for the *full punishment due.* This is the message we have received. It is the message that our world most needs to hear.

O God, give us the courage to proclaim it!

FOUR

BLOOD-EARNEST

Christian Courage to Stop the Shedding of Innocent Blood

Rescue those who are being taken away to death;
Hold back those who are stumbling to the slaughter.

– Proverbs 24:11

If you chose to resist evil and you chose it firmly, then ways of carrying out that resistance will open up around you. [24]

– André Trocmé

Infanticide in China.

Sati in India.

Twin killing in Africa.

Euthanasia in parts of Europe.

Abortion everywhere.

Throughout history, Christians the world over have been and continue to be routinely confronted with the shedding of innocent blood. What should we do?

In Vichy France during the 1940s, André Trocmé saw mothers and children fleeing death. He saw that many Christians of his day were prepared to do nothing in response. They "thought of themselves as meek and humble Christians, but they were actually cowards who failed to dare to live according to their own consciences."[19]

I do not want such things said of this generation of the Church. If the same spirit that raised Jesus from the dead lives in us, then we ought to be a people marked by our daring and courage to live according to our biblically informed conscience.

The word that has shaped my own conscience and prodded me to action more than any other is Proverbs 24:10-12.

> [10] If you faint in the day of adversity, your strength is small. [11] Rescue those who are being taken away to death; hold back those who are stumbling to the slaughter. [12] If you say, "Behold, we did not know this," does not he who weighs the heart perceive it? Does not he who keeps watch over your soul know it, and will he not repay man according to his work?

Let's walk through these three crucial verses together.

Verse 10 Chides and Dares Us

Proverbs 24:10-12 begins by chiding the spirit of fear: "If you faint in the day of adversity, your strength is small."

That sounds like a double-dog dare. God did not rescue us from sin and death to build a community of nervous chipmunks ever sniffing the air for potential danger. He sealed our lives with his own death-defying Spirit so that we might act in kind. Rather, "the righteous are bold as a lion" (Proverbs 28:1). If you react cowardly in times of trouble, you must think your God so small!

Cowardice is a serious matter. Do not confuse it with timidity or caution or even fear. *Cowardice is passive rebellion against what God calls us to stand for and do in this world.* This applies here, today, to the world you and I live in right now.

You can be cautious and afraid, yet with ever-whispering prayers for strength, obey God. The difference between the godly fearful and the cowardly fearful is that the cowardly do not finally obey. On the day of judgment, God deals with passive rebellion the same way he deals with the more active kind: "as for the *cowardly*, the faithless, the detestable, as for murderers, the sexually immoral, sorcerers, idolaters, and all liars, their portion will be in the lake that burns with fire and sulfur, which is the second death" (Revelation 21:8). I am not saying that cowardice will send a Christian to hell. I am saying we need to flee cowardice in the same way we need to flee sexual immorality and sorcery.

God is strong. Stand with him on the day of adversity.

Verse 11 Commands and Inspires Us

Things like divorce or sickness or bankruptcy are trials in their own way, but the trouble in view in Proverbs 24:10-12 is a deadly serious affair that, according to verse 11, involves innocent blood. "Rescue those who are being taken away to *death*; hold back those who are stumbling to the *slaughter.*"

If a school bus full of children veers off the road in front of you and flips over, you need only seconds to react.

At a minimum you grab a cell phone and dial 911. No command for action is needed when the death of innocents or the threat of their death is *accidental*. But verse 11 has *intentionality* in mind ("rescue those who are being *taken away* to death") and somehow in these cases we often need to be told what to do. Unless the ones committing the evil are obviously criminals, we may begin to hesitate. And the more established, accepted, powerful, entrenched, or institutionalized the evil, the less likely we are to act at all.

Verse 11 reminds us there are stark categories. Is an innocent one in danger of death? If so, then this is wrong, regardless of the surrounding circumstances, or how common it may be, or how widely it may be accepted. We must act to oppose it. The command brings clarity that inspires us and reminds us to do what is right.

The reality is that all around us, weaker people are being killed by more powerful people and forces. Against them and on behalf of the weak, God sends us forth: "*Rescue* those who are being taken away to death."

Obedience Takes Many Forms but Is Easily Recognized

How would we recognize obedience to the call of verse 11? If this word became flesh in us by the power of the Holy Spirit, what would it look like?

Reuben. In Shechem during the days of Jacob, it looked like Reuben. When all Joseph's other brothers wanted to kill him and tell their father that a wild animal had done it, Reuben—the eldest brother—saved Joseph's life. Reuben used persuasion and the Word of God to remind them of the sanctity of human life. "When Reuben heard it, he rescued him out of their hands, saying, 'Let us not take his life.' And Reuben said to them, 'Shed no blood…'" (Genesis 37:21-22).

The Egyptian midwives and Moses' mother. In Egypt during the days of Israel's bondage, it looked like the midwives. They used the courage of their faith to defy the child-killing policy of Pharaoh (Exodus 1:17). At the same time, Moses' mother used secrecy to save her son (2:2). When caring for him secretly was no longer possible, she provided him a home and later placed him for adoption with Pharaoh's daughter (2:10).

Rahab. In the days of conquest, obedience to verse 11 looked like Rahab. She used deception to rescue the spies from death (Joshua 2) and was commended (James 2:25).

Among the Israelites. In Saul's time, obedience took the form of a whole crowd of witnesses standing as one. "The people said to Saul, 'Shall Jonathan die…Far from it! As the Lord lives, there shall not one hair of his head fall to the ground, for he has worked with God this day.' So the people ransomed Jonathan, so that he did not die" (1 Samuel 14:45).

Obadiah. In the time of the prophets, obedience looked like Obadiah, who organized safe homes and sustainable care for 100 prophets to rescue them from Jezebel's slaughter (1 Kings 18:4).

Esther. During the exile it looked like Esther. She rescued her people from legally sanctioned genocide by working to change the law (Esther 4:14), endangering her own life in the process.

Shadrach, Meshach, and Abednego. In a variation on the theme of rescuing others, and a demonstration of the courage that comes from faith, these three innocent young men had no one to stand up for them and no resources to rely on. All they had to rescue themselves from death was prayer and the courage to die if that was what faithfulness to God required. "Our God whom we serve is able to deliver us from the burning fiery furnace, and he will deliver us out of your hand, O king. But if not, be it known…we will not serve your gods" (Daniel 3:17-18).

The early Church. During the first generation of the Church, rescue as described in Proverbs 24 took the form of pastoral leadership and disciple making, "teaching them to observe *all* that I have commanded you" (Matthew 28:20). *All* certainly included Christ's teaching to value life and personally intervene to stop the death of innocents (Luke 10:25-37). The early Church took Jesus' command to "go and do likewise" and applied it to their times. In the Roman world of those days, abortion, infanticide, exposure, and abandonment were common. The church leaders immediately set out to purge this practice from among themselves. They taught: "There are two different ways: the way of life and the way of death, and the difference between these two is great. Therefore, do not murder a child by abortion or kill a newborn infant."[20]

Then the Church went out to stop others from shedding innocent blood. They went to the city dumps and other places where babies were left to die and brought them into their own homes and adopted them. You should be proud of that. It is part of our Christian heritage.

India. In India during the turn of the 18th century, rescue took the form of James Peggs (1793-1850) and William Carey (1761-1834). Peggs served as a missionary south of Calcutta. Sati (or suttee), a form of self-immolation, was regularly pressed upon Hindu widows. They were burned alive with the corpses of their dead husbands as a sign of devotion and purity. Peggs, just as Hebrew 11:33 commends, labored to "enforce justice." He exposed the injustice and inhumanity of sati. He published *India's Cries to British Humanity, Relative to Infanticide, British Connection with Idolatry, Ghau Murders, Suttee, Slavery, and Colonization in India* in 1832. His book included an eyewitness account. [21]

William Carey (1761-1834) himself witnessed a sati in 1799. For 30 years he worked to abolish the practice. Finally, "On December 4, 1829, the necessary edict was signed and given to Carey to translate into Bengali, in order that it might be published in both languages." The message reached Carey on Sunday morning. "Throwing aside his quaint black coat, he exclaimed, 'No church for me today; if I delay an hour to translate and publish this, many a widow's life may be sacrificed.'" The authorities had the translation before evening."[22] This too is part of our heritage as believers. [23]

Africa. In Africa, obedience to Proverbs 24:11 looked like Mary Slessor (1848-1915). Mary learned that upon the death of a tribal chief or some other dignitary, random innocent people were selected for ritual killing. When she heard of a nearby instance where a chief's son had died, she ran to the village. She found about a dozen men and women who had been selected for poisoning, and confronted the chief.

The chief said he had somehow divined that the selected individuals were responsible for the death of his son and added, "If they are not guilty, the poison will not harm them." After many appeals, the chief freed some but was determined to murder the others. Mary Slessor fought for their lives with endless argument and testimony. The chief threatened her for interfering, but she testified that the God she served was strong and had sent her to fight for these souls. In the end, she carried the day.

But Mary wasn't finished. Twins were considered a curse in this part of Africa. Both babies were routinely slaughtered or put out in the brush to perish of hunger or to be eaten by ants or leopards. Mary determined to stop it.

The first set of twins she rescued, she adopted herself. But then, as she collected more, she needed an orphanage. Today, Mary Slessor of Calabar is renowned in Nigeria as *Eko Kpukpro Oura* (Mother of All People). Her unwavering strength and courage in rescuing the innocent won much of Nigeria to the Christian faith.

All of these stories, and so many others, comprise the spiritual DNA from which you and I descend in the Christian faith. There are endless accounts of people who mustered their courage and found ways to rescue innocent life. Just from these few examples we see that obedience can be manifested in a wide range of behaviors and approaches. Some involve small actions taken in private by single individuals. Others involve numerous people, visible and boldly active on the public stage for long periods of time. In each case, the particular form of obedience necessary will be shaped by the particular form of evil present in that season.

André Trocmé believed, "If you chose to resist evil and you chose it firmly, then ways of carrying out that resistance will open up around you."[24] What Christians have done down through history to resist the shedding of innocent blood, and how they did it, forms an endless line of splendor. Let us join the psalmist: "As for the saints who are in the land, they are the excellent ones, in whom is all my delight" (Psalm 16:3). And let us join those saints in the work.

Learning to Obey

But first we must ask, *how* did they do it? How did the saints of old find the means to obey God's call to rescue? How do we, in turn, obey this command in our own time?

We obey it the same way we obey all the commands of God—*by faith*. Consider Hebrews 11: 7 when it says Noah acted radically for the salvation of others: "By *faith* Noah, being warned by God concerning events as yet unseen, in reverent fear constructed an ark for the *saving* of his household." Noah rescued his family by faith—that is, *by the power, courage, and determination that his faith in God produced in him*.

How did Moses rescue the firstborn of Israel? "By *faith*, he kept the Passover and sprinkled the blood, so that the Destroyer of the firstborn might not touch them" (Hebrews 11:28).

How did Gideon, Barak, Samson, Jephthah, David, Samuel, and the prophets conquer kingdoms, enforce justice, obtain promises, stop the mouths of lions, quench the power of fire, escape the edge of the sword, find their weakness turned into strength, and more? All of them accomplished all of this "through faith" (Hebrews 11:33).

When you choose to take a stand against the shedding of innocent blood, you don't know exactly what will happen. How have Christians historically found the courage and the strength of character to accept a set of repercussions they cannot even define? People just like us have found such strength through faith in their great God.

> But recall the former days when, after you were enlightened, you endured a hard struggle with sufferings, 33 sometimes being publicly exposed to reproach and affliction, and sometimes being partners with those so treated. 34 For you had compassion on those in prison, and you joyfully accepted the plundering of your property, since you knew that you yourselves had a better possession and an abiding one. 35 Therefore do not throw away your confidence, which has a great reward. 36 For you have need of endurance, so that when you have done the will of God you may receive what is promised. (Hebrews 10:32-36)

Notice the links. After being enlightened (v 32), a reference to their new life in Christ, they endured suffering as a result of aiding those in prison (v 33). They even lost their homes. Where did this capacity for courageous compassion come from? From *believing* that God had preserved for them a better home in heaven (v 34).

This appears to me the whole point of Hebrews 11 — to give us more courage by pointing to the powerful things people do when they have faith in a mighty God. Again, when we are moved to take action, we cannot know the outcome. In the providence of God, we may suffer for the sake of righteousness or triumph in the name of Christ. Indeed, the two often go together. But each time our faith causes us to stand up against the shedding of innocent blood, our faith will also grant us boldness.

Everything we are called to stand for and fight for in this world is done by the same faith in the same God as those saints in Hebrews 11 had. We look to him who rescued us from sin and death, and then we run into the breach.

Saving faith saves others. This statement is no more radical than proclaiming that those who love God love their neighbors. Whether we call it faith in God or love for God, when we act courageously in the day of adversity, God is at work in us as a life-saving power. This faith dares to look at the death of the innocent and say, "Not on my watch! Not without a fight!"

In truth, the real battle we face on the day of trouble is not the imminent danger or the evil force. It is the fight of faith itself. Will we act with faith toward God or will we shrink back?

Verse 12 Warns and Emboldens Us

When you look at the long line of faithful witnesses mentioned in Hebrews 11 and read the biographies of those who lived boldly as people of conscience and purpose, then you cannot help but see faith and courage as nearly synonymous. To say these men and women were faithful is to say they *found* courage when it *took* courage to remain faithful to God. That is why I state with so much confidence that when we are faced with the shedding of innocent blood, courage is *required* of our faith. That is no different than saying that *faithfulness* is required of our faith. Courage is to faith what ice is to water: it is the form that faith takes when confronted with cold injustice. Faith hardens into courage.

Indeed, it must. Trouble often comes when we rescue those in the crosshairs of destruction. The record of history is fairly consistent here. Rescuers of the innocent have often suffered the same treatment as the victims they sought to defend.

One official, seeking Trocmé's cooperation in rounding up Jews, told him, "Monsieur Trocmé, you would do well to take care. If you are not prudent, it is you whom I shall be obliged to have deported. To the good listener, warning!"[25] Even if the situation you and I face is not nearly this oppressive, when we are confronted with the shedding of innocent blood, we will still tend to choose self-preservation over risk and uncertainty. God knows this about us. He even anticipates this being our first reaction. So in Proverbs 24:12, he calls it out so we will press through it toward courageous intervention. "If you say, 'Behold, we did not know this,' does not he who weighs the heart perceive it? Does not he who keeps watch over your soul know it, and will he not repay man according to his work?"

God knows that our first response to someone else being in danger is *not* to think in terms of the Golden Rule.[26] Apart from accidents, as I noted earlier, our first response to the endangerment of the innocent will nearly always be evasion or willful ignorance. Even when the situation carries minimal danger to us, so that all we would risk would be some time or money, avoidance is our natural first response. Jesus draws out this picture in his Samaritan Parable. The priest and the Levite "crossed over" from where the dying man lay: they did not want to *know* anything so that they did not have to *do* anything.

Two Responses to this Verse

Proverbs 24:12 pushes us to a dividing point of self-identification. That is, we will break into two camps based on how we respond to this verse.

Blinded by fog. If you are like most of us you will react poorly, at least at first. You will surround yourself with a protective fog generated from two sources: your own heart of self-preservation, and the general fog of denial and willful ignorance that rests thick and gray upon our entire culture. This fog will stand between you and two things that should be obvious: the simple clarity of the verses we have been studying in this chapter, and the fact that innocent blood is being shed.

In a fog, your vision is impaired. From within it you will conveniently be able to dodge the question of whether you *will* or *will not* intervene in the shedding of innocent blood. You will simply appeal to the dimness of your sight and thereby feign ignorance about what was needed in the moment of decision. You will say, "Look, I had no idea what was happening! I didn't know that it was a real life-and-death situation."

André Trocmé saw this playing out in France. He wrote, "Many French let themselves be deceived in 1942." Hallie draws out his meaning:

> This is a psychologically penetrating statement. The Chambonnaise under Trocmé on the other hand would not let themselves be deceived. Trocmé knew enough about Nazism and cared enough about its victims to realize that what the Germans were doing— whatever it was—was not for the good of the Jews. Perhaps he did not know more about Nazism than many other Frenchmen—Hitler's anti-Semitism was no secret in Europe—but he cared enough about its victims to realize what giving the Jews to the Germans meant for the Jews. [27]

So for one group of people, their first reaction to the shedding of innocent blood becomes their governing principle. These are the self-preserving. Like the priest and the Levite in the Samaritan Parable, they want to be uninformed. They prefer things to be foggy, because that way life can continue smoothly. From within their fog, both black and white can appear as any one of 1000 shades of gray, depending entirely on how thick the fog is at a given point.

This group loves the word *nuance*. It can be a powerful tool for maintaining the status quo and for justifying inaction and passivity. It is frequently also a self-important word, a means of convincing themselves that in the face of this allegedly complex question, they are the sophisticated thinkers, not one of the simpleminded. Their intellectual capacity allows them to perceive distinctions that others miss, distinctions that suggest to them either that innocent blood is not being shed, or that the shedding of innocent blood does not demand opposition.

All of this is self-preservation. All of it results from hiding within a moral fog.

God sees right through it. He exposes its vapidness. "Does not he who keeps watch over your soul know it, and will he not repay man according to his work?" Here, part of what God is saying is, "Even if you succeed in deceiving yourself about the slaughter of the innocent, do you really think you can hide your true motive from me? When you fool yourself, do you imagine you are fooling me as well?"

Emboldened by faith. On the other hand, there is also a call to faith in this verse. It is found in the words, "he who keeps watch over your soul." The heart of faith says, "I will trust in God to watch over me. I will entrust my well-being to his safe-keeping."

This is the response of the second group. This is the group that, on the basis of faith hardened into courage, recognizes that they can and must take action and accept risk for the sake of the innocent.

God is watching over your soul, your life. Therefore you can spend it. "The righteous are as bold as a lion" (Proverbs 28:1). Why? Because they know a lion-sized truth: "Whoever finds his life will lose it, and whoever loses his life for my sake will find it" (Matthew 10:39). God himself supplies us the courage to rescue the innocent by reminding us that we have put our faith in him and he will honor our expression of that faith.

Consider the closing words of this passage, "Will he not repay man according to his work?" This is not suggesting that when we act in defense of the innocent, we earn merit from God, and this *obligates* him to repay us. That is not how it works. Christians already enjoy God's favor as his adopted children, exclusively and entirely because of Christ's finished work on the cross. Rather, this verse tells us that when we step out of our comfort zone to defend the innocent, God is for us *in that act of faith*. It is not a matter of earning merit. It is simply that God is pleased with our tangible expression of trust in the one who keeps watch over our souls, and that pleasure produces rewards for us, rewards that may well be temporal, but are certainly eternal.

Of course, the flip side is also true: Shrink back from the call to rescue the innocent and you identify yourself as someone who believes that God is not trustworthy.

Which is it for you? Is God trustworthy, or isn't he?

Today's Threat, Today's Generation

May I offer a generalization about the present generation of Christians, by which I mean all Christians alive today in the Western world?

We are not a generation marked by the courage that comes from faith.

Trocmé said of his generation, "The Christian Church should drop to its knees and beg pardon of God for its present incapacity and cowardice."[28] Is this true of us as well, as we face the shedding of innocent blood that is abortion? John Piper is one pastoral leader who has openly wrestled with this question.

Many pastors surpass me in their courage and consistency. I praise God for them. I will happily honor their superior rewards in the last day. But oh, how I long to be among them. So when it comes to abortion, I try. So much more could be done. I agonize over what more I should do, and this is not the only such issue! But for fifteen awakened years I have done what I can.

I preach on the horrific sin and injustice of abortion and on the glory of the cause of life at least once a year in our church. I try to encourage the Sanctity of Human Life Task Force in our church in other ways. I call our people to dream of ways of being sacrificially involved in the pro-life efforts to make abortion unthinkable in our country. I glorify adoption and fan the flames of its spread in our church. I offer precious blood-bought forgiveness and hope to all the women and men in the congregation who have experienced or encouraged abortion. I speak and pray at pro-life gatherings outside abortion clinics and support crisis pregnancy centers with my presence and my money. In past days I have joined peaceful protests and been arrested numerous times and spent one night in jail. I have made my case for life before angry crowds, and before judges, and over lunch with an abortionist.

The point is this: I believe pastors should put their lives and ministries on the line on this issue. The cowardice of some pastors when it comes to preaching against abortion appalls me. Many treat the dismemberment of unborn humans as an untouchable issue on par with partisan politics. . . . The law of our land is immoral and unjust. That should be declared from tens of thousands of pulpits in America.[29]

May it be so. And may pulpits in China, Africa, Europe, and South America inspire millions more to add their voice and good works. Is this not the purpose of the Church? "The reason the Son of God appeared was to destroy the works of the devil" (1 John 3:8). May God embolden us to make abortion, like slavery, one of those worldly evils over which we see the triumph of the gospel.

The Underground Railroad of the 21st Century

The generalization I have just made regarding this generation of Christians is not, however, the last word. I hasten to add that much good work is underway. A season of change appears to me well begun. I say this with rejoicing and gratitude to God, but also with trepidation, for with respect to abortion, a choir of cynical scoffers is ever eager to paint an entirely bleak picture. Nevertheless, I honestly believe many good things are happening, and this makes me proud.

- Thousands of Christian women have joined the Silent No More Campaign. Under the banner of "I regret my abortion" they are telling their stories publicly.
- Tens of thousands of Christians in almost 300 US cities now assemble in the spring and fall for 40 days of public, corporate prayer and fasting outside our nation's abortion businesses. Called "40 Days for Life," this public witness is leading to hundreds of changed minds, not only among those seeking abortions, but among those working in the abortion industry.
- In 1991, there were about 2,200 abortion businesses in the US. As of May 2011, there were only 678, and it seems like every month I learn of another closing.
- Christian college students are standing for life in remarkable numbers these days, with more than 600 campuses now hosting Students for Life chapters.
- Forty years ago, there were no more than a dozen or two organized efforts to rescue pregnant mothers "stumbling to the slaughter." Today there are more than 3000 pregnancy help centers and maternity homes across the US and Canada. I know Christians in 49 other countries striving to establish similar movements, and surely there are others I am unaware of.

As I said before, to me this is nothing less than the Underground Railroad of our day. On one front, women, children, and couples are being rescued one at a time. On another front, people pray and work that our fellow citizens and representatives might come to see, with appropriate horror and revulsion, that abortion is a tragic smear against our own proclamation that all people have an inalienable right to life.

To my knowledge, all the good work I am referring to here has been developed by the Christian community at their own expense. It has all been done under the "lest innocent blood be shed" banner, and what's more the pregnancy-help movement has worked hard to maintain an evangelistic edge. This is the most winsome, life-saving, and life-changing response to the bloodguilt of abortion in the history of redemption. It may be the most evangelistic work of our time as well.

Martha Avila leads one of these efforts under the name Heartbeat of Miami. Her story is typical of how the pregnancy-help movement has grown. In 2006, she learned that about 35 abortion businesses plagued her city, most of them targeting predominantly Black and Latino neighborhoods. Martha helped build a team of nurses, doctors, counselors, mentors, and trainers to help young mothers choose life and prepare to parent their newborn children or place them for adoption. She raised the money needed to rent an office, buy an ultrasound machine, and build a staff so that, to whatever extent God would bless, she might save lives and win her neighborhood for Christ.

Cross-Bearing for the Child-Bearing

Every month Martha sends out another story of a life

saved and changed. Recently, I received the following account in which she writes quite naturally how the gospel of Christ and the gospel of life advance together, just as the Apostle seemed to expect when he said, "For we are to God the pleasing *aroma of Christ* among those who are being saved…an *aroma that brings life*" (2 Corinthians 2:15-16). Martha writes:

> *Terri, 31, came into our clinic seeking an abortion. She felt there was no way out of her situation. She had three children at home. She had just lost her job. The father of her baby, Ron, told her he could not handle it and moved out of town.*

> *For days she cried and prayed. God led her to our pregnancy help center instead of one of the many abortion businesses in our area. We confirm positive pregnancy tests with an ultrasound. To our surprise she was 15 weeks pregnant and there were **two** precious baby boys in her womb! Terri was in shock. She watched the babies on the screen. One sucked his thumb and then appeared to put his other hand on his brother's arm. Terri cried, "My babies cannot die. But two will be impossible." Jesse, her counselor, told her, "Nothing is impossible for God."*

> *Terri chose life for her babies in spite of having no idea how she would do it. We prayed for her and assured her we would continue to seek ways to help her.*

On a follow-up call Jesse found Terri exhausted and scared. She still had no job. Now the rent money was due. The babies' father was nowhere to be found. Jesse assured her that there were people in our community that loved life and loved her even though they did not know her personally. These were the same people who enabled us to give her a free ultrasound. One of them is Joan who works at our Respect Life office. They found the funds needed to pay Terri's rent.

We kept finding one piece of help at a time through our Christian social network. Terri could not believe that ordinary people, free of charge, joined together to help.

A month later, just when Terri had to pay her rent again, Ron returned with a repentant heart ready to take responsibility for his family. He was of course shocked to hear the news of the twins, but he embraced the situation wholeheartedly.

God's compassion for Terri and her babies were a result of her obedience. "As a father has compassion on his children, so the Lord has compassion on those who fear Him" (Psalm 103:13).

Martha signed her letter, "Cross-bearer for the child-bearer."

FIVE

BLOOD-WAR

Satan's Plan to Delay the Final Triumph of the Gospel

The dragon stood before the woman who was about to give birth, so that when she bore her child he might devour it.
— Revelation 12:4

The abortion holocaust is an evil torn free of its moorings in reason and causality, an ordinary secular corruption raised to unimaginable powers of magnification and limitless extremity.
— Bernard Nathanson [30]

Life is war.

In fighting for life, both innocent life and eternal life, we wage a war of love against dark forces that destroy body and soul. This war is cosmic in scope and, like labor pains, increasingly intense. For us who believe, it is a perilous, long-suffering, Christ-exalting fight. It will issue forth eventually in the ultimate triumph of the gospel, the return of Christ, a final judgment, and a new heaven and earth. Then we will rest. Until then, we are engaged in a great struggle.

Even though this war is spiritual in nature, sometimes you can almost smell the smoke of the battlefield. This week I received the following email about my friends in China, Zhang and Mai. [31] It reminds me of the tenacity that love demands of us, lest innocent blood be shed.

Zhang and his wife, Mai, went to their doctor's office. While waiting, they spotted another young couple in the waiting room. Mai turned to Zhang and said, "I think they're going to have an abortion." She prodded Zhang to say something.

Seeing the young man walk outside for a smoke, Zhang followed, started chatting, and eventually found out that they were indeed going to have an abortion. He pleaded with the man for quite some time—told him everything he'd learned about the baby being a life. The man even admitted it was a life.

Zhang even ran back home, grabbed his computer, ran back, and showed this couple the human life video you gave them. They wouldn't look. The wife was turning her back, totally ignoring their pleas. Zhang spoke very directly to him. The man (a chef) even told Zhang that his restaurant is above another abortion business. He saw the remains of children tossed into the trash and had to drink himself drunk to try to forget what he saw. Zhang told him his child would be just the same...

After much pleading, it appears the couple went ahead with the abortion. But the man especially (and by the end the woman, too) was very challenged by Zhang's pleading and exhortations. Zhang told him at one point they were doing this because they followed Jesus, they were Christians, and they valued all life. The man was so moved he gave Zhang his phone number. Zhang and Mai are going to follow up with them.

They were heart-broken when they told us, saying that they'd failed. But I reminded them what you told me, that couples who have abortions need the gospel now more than ever.

Bravo! Zhang and Mai are cross-bearing for the child-bearing. This is how you wage the war of love. You fight for the weak, in the name of Jesus. And you fight for the guilty, in the name of Jesus.

We Are Part of a Great Struggle

Revelation 12 has something to say about this war. The chapter is full of imagery and things difficult to understand. Nonetheless, it is for good reason that it appears in a book called Revelation, for there God calls us to present awareness and action:

By revealing the spiritual realities lying behind the church's trials and temptations during the time between Christ's first and second comings, and by dramatically affirming the certainty of Christ's

triumph in the new heaven and earth, the visions
granted to John both warn the church and fortify it
to endure suffering and to stay pure from the defiling
enticements of the present world order. [32]

In drawing to a conclusion this brief study of
innocent blood and the call to challenge the powers of
death with the gospel of life, I am particularly affected
by Revelation 12 and the blood-war it reveals. I think it
exposes a connection between the shedding of innocent
blood and the worldwide advance of the gospel. I believe
it speaks specifically to a link between killing innocent
children and the fulfillment of the Great Commission.

Do you believe there are spiritual forces arrayed
against the purposes of God in this world, by which I
mean the gospel and all that it entails? Do you believe that
those gospel-opposing spiritual forces will place particular emphasis on particular areas? And will not those areas
be "wedge issues," issues especially capable of dividing
human beings from God, the gospel, and one another by
targeting our greatest vulnerabilities?

If you answered yes to all three questions, then
consider an analogy that will help demonstrate the link
between the shedding of innocent blood and the progress
of the Great Commission.

<u>Pornography targets the gospel by targeting
marriage.</u> The vast, ever-growing, and obscenely prof-
itable pornography industry has the full support and
encouragement of the powers of darkness. Why? Because
it appeals to our sin nature in ways that uniquely weaken

our ability to form and maintain a God-glorifying marriage. The industry is an ongoing, escalating, full-bore assault on all present and future marriages—and this has significant negative repercussions for the spread of the gospel.

Abortion targets the gospel by eliminating many who would spread it. In exactly the same way, as horrific and wicked as abortion is in itself, for the enemy of our souls it is primarily a means to a greater end—the delay of the spread of the gospel. Revelation 12 reveals that Satan uses the mass weapon of child-killing to forestall the progress of the gospel. If this is true, then the conclusion is unavoidable. Abortion, the most prevalent form of child-killing, may well be Satan's chief weapon against world-evangelization today.

If this seems a startling conclusion, I can only ask you to consider Revelation 12:

> And a great sign appeared in heaven: a woman clothed with the sun, with the moon under her feet, and on her head a crown of twelve stars. She was pregnant and was crying out in birth pains and the agony of giving birth. And another sign appeared in heaven: behold, a great red dragon, with seven heads and ten horns, and on his heads seven diadems. His tail swept down a third of the stars of heaven and cast them to the earth. And the dragon stood before the woman who was about to give birth, so that when she bore her child he might devour it. She gave birth to a male child, one who is to rule all the nations with a

rod of iron, but her child was caught up to God and to his throne, and the woman fled into the wilderness, where she has a place prepared by God, in which she is to be nourished for 1,260 days.

Now war arose in heaven, Michael and his angels fighting against the dragon. And the dragon and his angels fought back, but he was defeated, and there was no longer any place for them in heaven. And the great dragon was thrown down, that ancient serpent, who is called the devil and Satan, the deceiver of the whole world—he was thrown down to the earth, and his angels were thrown down with him. And I heard a loud voice in heaven, saying, "Now the salvation and the power and the kingdom of our God and the authority of his Christ have come, for the accuser of our brothers has been thrown down, who accuses them day and night before our God. And they have conquered him by the blood of the Lamb and by the word of their testimony, for they loved not their lives even unto death. Therefore, rejoice, O heavens and you who dwell in them! But woe to you, O earth and sea, for the devil has come down to you in great wrath, because he knows that his time is short!"

And when the dragon saw that he had been thrown down to the earth, he pursued the woman who had given birth to the male child. But the woman was given the two wings of the great eagle so that she might fly from the serpent into the wilderness, to the place where she is to be nourished for a time, and times, and half a time. The serpent poured water like a river out of his mouth after the woman, to sweep her away with a flood. But the earth came to the help of the woman, and the earth opened its mouth and swallowed the river that the dragon had poured from his mouth. Then the dragon became furious with the woman and went off to make war on the rest of her offspring, on those who keep the commandments of God and hold to the testimony of Jesus. And he stood on the sand of the sea.

You do not need to understand everything in the chapter to grasp the larger point: we are engaged in a great struggle. This struggle is principally between God and Satan. It is a struggle between good and evil, between life and death.

This struggle started long ago—before the world was formed and populated—and every generation down through the ages and across every culture and language, down to this generation and this hour, is part of this one great struggle. The battlefield stretches into the heavenly realms. But woe to us! Satan has been thrown down to the earth. His war against God is extended to the people of God. The result is suffering and death for all peoples in every age, especially "those who keep the commandments of God and hold to the testimony of Jesus."

The Gospel as War

After Satan enticed Adam to join him in breaking faith with God, God announced his plan to fight for life and to wage a war of love against the powers of death. He said to Satan, "I will put enmity between you and the woman, and between your offspring and her offspring; he shall bruise your head, and you shall bruise his heel" (Genesis 3:15). That is, Satan will strike a painful blow on this promised offspring, but this promised one will deliver a deadly blow (thus the comparison between head and heel).

Satan struck hard on the day of Jesus' crucifixion. He thought he had dealt a deadly blow to God's plan. Yet his exultation soon turned to bitterness and wrath, for although Christ suffered and died on the cross, that death sealed Satan's defeat.

Now, knowing that Christ won an inevitable victory at the cross, Satan is driven by a single terrifying reality — the culmination of his own fatal bruising approaches. God is sovereign over time. To him it is a trivial matter. "With the Lord one day is as a thousand years, and a thousand years as one day" (2 Peter 3:8). But Satan is bound to time and obsessed with it. All that he does, all his schemes and devices, are calculated now to buy more of it: "because he knows his time is short" (Revelation 12:12).

Today, and every day until the return of Christ, Satan combines his hatred and his genius, not merely to fight against God and his people, but to fight in a way that delays the gospel from reaching its global and historic fullness. [33]

The Gospel as World History

God created the world for the purpose of the gospel of the Son of God. "All things were created through him and for him" (Colossians 1:16). History is like a canvas for Christ. The events of history are the brush strokes, the layering of colors and textures by which the glory of God in the face of Christ gradually appears and is magnified in the world (however slowly, from our limited perspective, this may seem to happen).

God unveiled the outlines of his worldwide plan of redemption in Christ to Abraham:

> And I will make of you a great nation, and I will bless you and make your name great, so that you will be a blessing. I will bless those who bless you, and him who dishonors you I will curse, and in you all the families of the earth shall be blessed. (Genesis 12:2-3)

While history unfolds in myriad ways, all of it tying to the promise God made to Abraham, the Bible records that history as it relates most directly to this promise. So we learn in Scripture how the nation of Israel was established: the people are enslaved in Egypt, and after 400 years of bondage, God sends them a savior, Moses, who delivers them out of their misery and leads them to the promised land where God dwells in their midst as sovereign ruler. The moral imperative underlying God's promise to the Israelites is repeated in each generation: "Trust him and it well go well with you."

This history of Israel sets up the greater history that is to yet to be fully realized—deliverance by a great Savior from the bondage of sin and death, a Savior who leads his people into the promised land of a new heaven and earth where the Savior himself lives and reigns among his people, to their unending joy.

Many centuries into this developing history of redemption, David prays for God's blessing upon Israel, that Israel might prove to be a blessing of salvation to all peoples.

> May God be gracious to us and bless us
> and make his face to shine upon us,
> that your way may be known on earth,
> *your saving power among all nations.*
> Let the peoples praise you, O God;
> let *all the peoples* praise you!
> Let *the nations* be glad and sing for joy,
> for you judge the peoples with equity
> and guide the nations upon earth.
> Let the peoples praise you, O God;
> let *all the peoples* praise you! (Psalm 67:1-3)

But Israel breaks faith with God. They suffer for their sins and experience the righteous judgments of the Lord. Nonetheless, for the sake of his own promise, God does not destroy Israel completely. As the Old Testament comes to a close, and the chosen people lie humbled, God affirms his Abrahamic promise: "For from the rising of the sun to its setting my name will be great among the nations, and in every place incense will be offered to my name, and a pure offering. For my name will be great among the nations, says the Lord of hosts" (Malachi 1:11).

In the fullness of time, Christ is born. His incarnation, life, death, and resurrection inaugurate the "end times" when the promised blessing of redemption becomes the power of conversion and transformation, for the Jew first and then spreading quickly to all peoples (Acts 2:17, 1 Corinthians 10:11). Thus, what Christ purchased on the cross, he sends his disciples out to collect: "Go therefore and make disciples of *all nations* (Matthew 28:28). On the day of Pentecost he gives them his Spirit, and by that Spirit he gives an experience emblematic of what will unfold in subsequent generations—Christ's disciples will go forth and people from many nations will hear the gospel in their own language and rejoice in it (Acts 2:1-11).

If the day of Pentecost points to the *beginning* of the end times (the consummation of all things), then the fulfillment of the Great Commission will mark the *end* of the end times, as the promise made long ago to Abraham becomes a living reality. This is what heaven rejoices in!

> Worthy are you to take the scroll and to open its seals, for you were slain, and by your blood you ransomed people for God from *every tribe and language and people and nation*, and you have made them a kingdom and priests to our God, and they shall reign on the earth. (Revelation 5:9-10)

Again, when God completes the great work of the gospel, what will we see? We will see the promise to Abraham fulfilled.

> After this I looked, and behold, a great multitude that no one could number, *from every nation, from*

all tribes and peoples and languages, standing before the throne and before the Lamb, clothed in white robes, with palm branches in their hands, and crying out with a loud voice, "Salvation belongs to our God who sits on the throne, and to the Lamb!" (Revelation 7:9-10)

Then will come the end of this world as we know it. God will perfect the establishment of his kingdom and complete his victory in the blood-war by consummating his judgment against Satan. That dreadful day of judgment is precisely what moves Satan to plot woe upon the world. Whatever brings that day closer, Satan is hell-bent on targeting and destroying.

Satan Attacks the Innocent to Impede the Gospel

Fearing the lake of fire (Revelation 20:10), Satan must try to stop the church from acting like a people forgiven and set free. He must seek to prevent us from doing the good works God has prepared for us to do (Ephesians 2:10).

The apostle Paul said, "we are not ignorant of his designs" (2 Corinthians 2:11). Paul did not mean we can always know specifically what the devil is doing, only that we *can* know his general mode of operation everywhere and at all times. Primarily, Satan leverages our own sin to blunt our witness and impact.

When Paul wrote to the Ephesians about not being ignorant of Satan's ways, he had in mind unforgiveness between believers. He knew that sustained unforgiveness is like inviting an infestation by leaving food out on the counter each night. In the same way, unforgiveness attracts and invites Satanic opportunity. So Paul extends forgiveness to the Corinthians and urges their forgiveness of one another, "so that we would not be outwitted by Satan; for we are not ignorant of his designs" (2 Corinthians 2:11). Among his many designs, Satan can and will use oppression, greed, corruption, and division within and among Christians. If he thinks it will disable us, distract us, or put us to sleep, he will try to use it.

One of his designs, used repeatedly throughout history to stop the progress of the gospel, is child-killing. We ought not to be ignorant of this design. For while Satan can be cunning, at times he is simply brutal, and his brutal use of the blunt weapon of child-killing is what Revelation 12:4 portrays: "And the dragon stood before the woman who was about to give birth, so that when she bore her child he might devour it."

Assault on the baby Jesus. Satan sought to stop the progress of the gospel by devouring Christ as an infant. We see this played out through Herod. As Satan's pawn, Herod saw the threat that the newborn king represented and sought to kill (devour) him. In a demonic fury, Herod "sent and killed all the male children in Bethlehem and in all that region who were two years old or under" (Matthew 2:16). *Why wait till he grows up and grows strong? Kill him while he is weak and defenseless*, we can imagine Herod (and Satan) thinking.

Satan was only after the One Child, but he was willing to unleash a weapon of mass child-killing to get him, as the inconsolable grief of the mothers of Bethlehem can testify.

Assault on the baby Moses. This was not the first time mass child-killing had been used to stop the progress of the gospel. Moses, of course, was targeted in much the same way. God elected Moses to deliver the people of Israel from the bondage of Egypt. Moses' life and work therefore represented a seismic step forward in the unfolding plan of redemption.

Satan set out to devour Moses when he was a weak and vulnerable newborn, before he could boldly live out God's will for his life. Satan doesn't know anymore than we do whom God will save or whom he will call to accomplish things great or small for his kingdom. So Satan set out to kill *all* the baby boys in order to kill the *one* baby boy. At first, Pharaoh ordered the Jews to kill their own babies. When they refused, he called on the Egyptian people to target them for infanticide (Exodus 1:16, 22).

Some public policies do come from the pit of hell.

Assault on God's justice. Later in Israel's history, Satan sought to trap God in his own justice. He sought to force God to destroy Israel for their wickedness. To accomplish this he again turned to child-killing. He induced Israel to commit child-sacrifice, something so utterly profane and insulting to a holy and loving God that he himself calls it unthinkable: "They built the high places of Baal in the Valley of the Son of Hinnom, to offer up their sons and daughters to Molech, though I did not command them, *nor did it enter into my mind,* that they should do this abomination, to cause Judah to sin" (Jeremiah 32:35).

This surely did anger God. But for the sake of his promise, he did not destroy Israel completely, delaying his full wrath until the day he poured it out on his Son.

God Rescues the Innocent to Advance the Gospel

In his war against God and the divine plan of redemption, Satan, as we have seen, repeatedly attacks innocent babies. But our God is a rescuing God. In Revelation 12 he moves to save the woman and the baby:

> And when the dragon saw that he had been thrown down to the earth, he pursued the woman who had given birth to the male child. But the woman was given the two wings of the great eagle so that she might fly from the serpent into the wilderness, to the place where she is to be nourished for a time, and times, and half a time. (Revelation 12:13)

Foiled by the rescuing power of God, the dragon strikes again, spewing a river of water at the woman and her child in an enraged effort to destroy them. But God comes to the woman's rescue again by causing the earth to open up and swallow what was sent forth to devour (12:15-16).

Satan seeks to devour, but God comes to rescue. We see it over and over. Satan whispered into Pharaoh's ear, and later into Herod's, saying, "Kill." Each time, God intervened. He gave a defiant courage to the midwives in Egypt. He instructed Joseph in a dream to take Mary and Jesus and flee from the murderous plan unfolding in Bethlehem.

But Satan is not so easily dissuaded. Even after God himself protects the woman, Satan continues his attacks: "Then the dragon became furious with the woman and went off to *make war* on the rest of her offspring, on those who keep the commandments of God and hold to the testimony of Jesus" (Revelation 12:17). This means Satan is unchanged in his *intent*. As we look back on how Satan has made war in the past, and compare it to the evidence we see today, we have every reason to believe he is similarly unchanged in one of his primary *tactics* — he is still targeting the defenseless.

Today, there are more tools and opportunities than ever before to spread the gospel to every corner of the globe. The more that gospel spreads, the closer Satan comes to the lake of fire. But it takes *people* to complete the Great Commission; in the task of disciple-making, technology will never outperform the radiant power of a person living according to the commands of God and bearing testimony to the grace of Christ. From Satan's perspective, every child who comes to birth may grow to be one more Christ-follower. Why would he not use the weapon of mass child-killing called abortion to sweep away as many people as possible in order to forestall the progress of the gospel?

Abortion and World Missions

Abortion sweeps away about 42 million babies a year. By any measure, abortion is the greatest weapon of mass destruction ever unleashed.

If 42 million 2-year-olds were being slaughtered every

year, our lives would be ordered around the horror of it. Try to imagine that—whatever policies or laws might be used to try to justify the death of *123,000 toddlers every day*, even atheists would call it deeply evil. And all Christians would be able to see, without qualification or reservation, that satanic powers were at work in and through these laws and policies. Moreover, we would instantly grasp how such a demonic weapon was nothing less than a blood-war against life itself, and an assault on the kingdom of God. We would all understand that among those 42 million lost every year were many who would otherwise grow up to testify to God's grace and pour themselves into the great work of the gospel. That we *do not* react to abortion in this same way is part of what makes it so supremely evil.

The late Dr. Bernard Nathanson helped legalize abortion in America. It was a cunning plan that he lived to regret and renounce.[34] Watching how Christians fought for life, he turned to Christ for the bloodguilt of 60,000 abortions that he performed.[35] He wrote:

> The abortion holocaust is beyond the ordinary discourse of morality and rational condemnation. It is not enough to pronounce it absolutely evil. . . . The abortion tragedy is a new event, severed from con- nections with traditional presuppositions of history, psychology, politics and morality. It extends beyond the deliberations of reason, beyond the discernment of moral judgment, beyond meaning itself. . . . This is an evil torn free of its moorings in reason and

causality, an ordinary secular corruption raised to unimaginable powers of magnification and limitless extremity. [36]

This devouring of children has become a global epidemic over the last 40 years while we have simultaneously seen a massive rise in missions research, consultation, collaboration, training, and agreed-upon goals dedicated to completing the Great Commission as far as we understand it. I do not believe this is a mere coincidence. Christians are hearing the Proverbs 24 call, seeing the connection between rescuing the innocent and evangelizing the lost, and they are responding.

During the week I finished this book, my 81-year-old mother jetted to Russia for two weeks of mission work, my daughter returned home to raise long-term support for her work among Muslims in Asia, my teenage nephew began preparing for his second short-term mission trip to Bolivia, and my niece began considering use of her training as a nurse for a medical missions trip to Africa. A passion for missions blows through our extended family. None of these relatives live near each other, but they are all answering a call to missions that is being trumpeted from many places, through many voices. Glory!

In China, during the last 40 years, the church has grown and multiplied faster than at any time or place in the history of redemption. By most estimates there are now 100 to 120 million believers there. While no one can say for sure what God has in mind for the church in China, many leaders there believe that God wants to use them to complete the Great Commission. They see how the gospel moved primarily west through Europe and Africa, across to the Americas, and in these last days, into Asia. They talk openly about Chinese believers assuming responsibility to bring the gospel to the Muslims of the Middle East and then "back to Jerusalem,"[37] thus circling the entire globe with the gospel of the risen Savior.

Yet at the same time, the Chinese, including many Chinese Christians, are killing their own babies in numbers far too large for us to register emotionally. There are 35,000 abortions every day in China.[38] Under the worst public policy in the history of mankind, some 13 million babies are swept away to death each year. Because the Chinese people for the past 30 years have only been allowed one child (and a birth permit is needed even for the one), boys are preferred. The One Child policy therefore breeds gendercide, both in the womb and even after birth: the ratio of boys to girls at birth is 120:100, though in some areas it runs as high as 163:100. As I mentioned earlier in this book, the Chinese government boasts that their One Child policy has resulted in 400 million fewer births in the last 30 years, as well as 500 female suicides a day.[39]

So in the time and place where we see unprecedented growth of the church and a growing passion to complete the task of world evangelization, we also see a law coercing parents to murder their children—each one a potential contributor to the spread of the gospel—in numbers never witnessed before.

If Satan used mass child-killing in Egypt to target the

one child called Moses and again in Bethlehem to target the one child called Jesus, why not use it today to target those among the unborn who would grow up to help complete the Great Commission? Forty-two million children wiped out every year before their first breath is a plan rightly called satanic. What is there to oppose it? Only one thing: Christians aflame with the moral courage that comes from faith in Jesus Christ, devoted to doing God's will. If we, like the midwives of Egypt, will commit our lives to God's safe keeping and get into the fight for life in the name of Christ, we can conquer Satan's plan.

And they have conquered him by the blood of the Lamb and by the word of their testimony, for they loved not their lives even unto death (Revelation 12:11).

SIX THINGS YOU CAN DO TO HELP SAVE THE INNOCENT

Learn to think clearly. Start by reading and listening.

READ

Third Time Around: A History of the Pro-Life Movement from the First Century to the Present, George Grant (Wolgemuth and Hyatt, 1991)

> *Inspired me to see that what we need to do is not new—it is just our turn.*

Aborted Women, Silent No More, David C. Reardon (Crossway Books, 1987)

> *Abortion is not an issue; it is a trauma. Women experience abortion more like a car crash than a personal choice. They <u>resort to it</u> and <u>yield to it</u> far more than choose it. This helps explain why the pregnancy help ministry has become the most lifesaving and evangelistic movement in America. See also <u>AfterAbortion.org.</u>*

The Case For Life: Equipping Christians to Engage the Culture , Scott Klusendorf, (Crossway Books, 2009)

> *The best rational, philosophical, and apologetical*

> *book on the sanctity of human life and abortion*
> *I know of. Scott speaks before college audiences*
> *regularly, debates the top defenders of legal abortion,*
> *and has honed the case for life to a fine point. See also*
> *ProLifeTraining.com.*

LISTEN

"Abortion, Race, Gender and Christ" (a sermon by John Piper) DesiringGod.org/resource-library/sermons/abortion-race-gender-and-christ#/listen/full

"When is Abortion Racism?" (a sermon by John Piper) DesiringGod.org/resource-library/sermons/when-is-abortion-racism#/listen/full

> *For 30 years, John Piper has marked the Martin*
> *Luther King holiday and the Sanctity of Human Life*
> *Sunday by addressing the most painful and sensitive*
> *issues of racism and abortion. All these sermons are*
> *worth your time (they can also be read at the Desiring*
> *God site), but these two show how abortion and a*
> *diminished view of human life feed into one another*
> *and call for a courageous response.*

Then begin to act.

PRAY

Join 40 Days for Life in your community.

> *Public and corporate prayers of lamentation and*
> *intercession often precede periods of spiritual*
> *awakening, social transformation, and mission*

advancement. Recently, another wave of prayer has arisen — this one seeking the triumph of the gospel of life over abortion. Find out where and when Christians are gathering in your community by going to 40DaysforLife.com.

TESTIFY

Testify personally: "I regret my abortion."

Christ in you is the aroma of life! Men and women who break the silence and shame that comes with paying for or submitting to abortion glorify the gospel, call others out of their own shame, and give hope to young people who are secretly on the precipice themselves. See also SilentNoMoreAwareness.org.

SUPPORT

Serve and Support the Pregnancy Help Movement.

Heartbeat International trains Christians to be lifesavers. This is the organization I turned to 20 years ago to learn how my family and local church could help women and couples choose life, prepare to parent, or place for adoption. They taught us what to say to those in crisis, how to locate the closest pregnancy help ministry, and how to start a new one. A few years ago I joined their staff to help spread the pregnancy help movement globally. Visit us at HeartbeatInternational.org.

CONNECT

Answer the call for help.

> *Almost every person considering abortion tells someone. When you are the one being confided in, you may not know what to say or do, but you can start here: Connect your friend or neighbor to a trained pregnancy help counselor, who will triage the situation and provide a connection to a nearby pregnancy help center.*
>
> *Option Line is a 24/7/365 hotline with a living, loving woman ready to help expectant mothers find God's provision for them and their babies. Visit <u>OptionLine.org</u> or call 1-800-395-HELP (4357).*

To get a free QR Reader:
1. Text SPARQ to 41411
2. Install and launch reader
3. Snap picture of QR Code

Endnotes

1. Phillip Hallie, *Lest Innocent Blood Be Shed* (HarperPerennial, 1994), 3.
2. André Trocmé, quoted in Hallie, 194.
3. The cross justifies God's mercy towards repentant sinners no matter when they lived. Their faith in the hope of atonement was counted as righteousness (Romans 4:3). This did create a problem, however. Prior to the cross, God's mercy to people

like Job or Abraham appeared as favoritism: it appeared that he was giving them a pass for their sins, but he was not. He delayed their just punishment and Christ justified his grace in their lives by suffering for their sins, too. The cross of Christ "was to show God's righteousness, because in his divine forbearance he had passed over former sins. It was to show his righteousness at the present time, so that he might be just and the justifier of the one who has faith in Jesus" (Romans 3:25). For more see, John Ensor, *The Great Work of the Gospel* (Crossway Books, 2006).

4. For more, see Alvin Schmidt's excellent book, *How Christianity Changed the World* (Zondervan, 2004).

5. Herbert Kretzmer, "Who Am I?" from *Les Misérables*, 1987.

6. A well documented review of the case can be found at http://www.npr.org/templates/story/story.php?storyId=129025516.

7. While we do not know for a fact whether Shipp and Smith committed crimes, they were clearly denied any semblance of due process under the law, and thus we can count them as innocents. Many other lynching victims were more clearly innocent.

8. It is also a word that has been adopted into Western legal codes.

9. I used this same analogy in *The Great Work of the Gospel* (Crossway Books, 2006) where I explore the wrath of God as a necessary part of his perfect love (see page 53).

10. It is not the taking of human life per se that is evil, but the *unlawful* taking. Christian leaders I resepct have argued that a high regard for human life means that capital punishment should be banned. This is not what I see in Scripture. Nevertheless, wherever we see a low regard for justice, we should be particularly slow to practice capital punishment: "You shall not pervert the justice due to your poor in his lawsuit. Keep far from a false charge, and do not kill the innocent and righteous, for I will not acquit the wicked" (Exodus 23:6-7).

Where the strict rules of justice cannot be insured—and there are many times and places where that is the case—then capital punishment should be suspended. In times of war or revolution, courts have often been set up as a cover for revenge or to remove opposition. When the prejudices of the times pressure judges to suspend or enforce the rules of evidence according to the outcome desired by the community, the courts then become guilty of shedding innocent blood. When a culture of corruption permeates a judicial system, we are facing one of those times when courage is required of our faith. There will be great pressure to remain silent. May God grant us courage.

11. See also Matthew 22:34-40, Luke 10:25-28.

12. If the message of the cross sounds too good to be true, the resurrection is our assurance that it is true. Jesus is "declared to be the Son of God in power according to the Spirit of holiness by his resurrection from the dead" (Romans 1:4). The resurrection is Christ's own vindication (see 1 Timothy 3:16).

13. For Facts on Induced Abortion Worldwide, Feb, 2011. See: http://www.guttmacher.org/pubs/fb_IAW.html

14. For Facts on Induced Abortion in the United States, May 2011 see: http://www.guttmacher.org/pubs/fb_induced_abortion.html

15. For research summary see: http://afterabortion.org/2011/abortion-risks-a-list-of-major-psychological-complications-related-to-abortion/

16. Martin Luther, quoted in Francis A. Schaeffer, *No Final Conflict* (InterVarsity Press, 1979), 13

17. "Has China's One-Child Policy Worked?" BBC News, accessed August 14, 2011, http://news.bbc.co.uk/2/hi/7000931.stm.

18. http://www.womensrightswithoutfrontiers.org/index.php?nav=female_suicide

19. Hallie, 90

20. Clayton Jefford, ed., *The Didache in Context, Essays on Its Text, History and Transmission* (E.J. Brill, 1995), 1.1 and 2.2.

21. James Peggs, *India's Cries to British Humanity, Relative to Infanticide, British Connection with Idolatry, Ghau Murders, Suttee, Slavery, and Colonization in India* (London: Simkin and Marshall, Stationers' Court, 1832), quoted by "Women in World History," accessed August 14, 2011, http://chnm.gmu.edu/wwh/p/106.html. Peggs included the account of Reverend J. England who witnessed this sati in southern India in June 1826: "I received a note from a gentleman that a *Suttee* was about to take place near his house. On hastening to the spot, I found the preparations considerably advanced. . . . On my right, sat the poor deluded widow, who was to be the victim of

this heart-rending display of Hindoo purity and gentleness; she was attended by a dozen or more Brahmuns; her mother, sister, and son (an interesting boy of about three years of age), and other relatives were also with her. Her own infant, now twelve months old, was craftily kept from her by the Brahmuns. . . . and everything about her person and her conduct indicated that narcotics had been administered in no small quantities. . . . Five or six Brahmuns began to talk to her with much vehemence, till, in a paroxysm of desperation, assisted by the Brahmuns, the hapless widow ascended the bed of destruction. Her mother and her sister stood by, weeping and agonized; but all was in vain—the blood-thirsty men prevailed. . . . her mother and sister, unable any longer to sustain the extremity of their anguish, went up to the side of the pile, and entreated that the horrid purpose might be abandoned; but the woman fearing the encounter, without uttering a word, or even casting a parting glance at her supplicating parent and sister, threw herself down on the pile, and clasped the half-putrid corpse in her arms. . . . the whole blazed . . . and covered the lifeless corpse and the living woman! A piercing sound caught my ear; I listened a few seconds, and, notwithstanding the noise of the multitude, heard the shrieks of misery which issued from the burning pile."

22. Copied by Stephen Ross for WholesomeWords.org from *Christian Heroism in Heathen Lands* by Galen B. Royer. Elgin, Ill.: Brethren Publishing House, 1915. http://www.wholesomewords.org/missions/bcarey3.html

23. Stephen Ross transcribed this story from Galen B. Royer's *Christian Heroism in Heathen Lands* (Elgin, Illinois: Brethren Publishing House, 1915) for WholesomeWords.org, accessed August 14, 2011, http://www.wholesomewords.org/missions/bcarey3.html.

24. Hallie, 92

25. Hallie, 103

26. However, if in a context of reliance upon God's grace, we were to train ourselves with the Golden Rule as soldiers train for battle, it would be sufficient.

27. Hallie, 104

28. Hallie, 171

29. John Piper, *Brothers, We Are Not Professionals,* (Broadman & Holman, 2002), 211-212

30. Bernard Nathanson, "Pro-Choice 1990," *New Dimensions,* October 1990, 38

31. Not their real names.

32. Introduction to Revelation, *ESV Study Bible,* accessed August 14, 20011, http://www.esvstudybible.org/images/excerpt-revelation-intro.pdf.

33. There is a sense in which neither Satan and his forces, nor human government with all their power, nor the wicked, nor any of us with our human sinful nature can thwart God's plans. God is sovereign. "He does all that he pleases" (Psalm 115:3). Who, after all, "can resist his will?" (Romans 9:19). A full answer requires more space, but when it comes to God's sovereign will, no one can know it let alone resist it successfully. Since the garden of Eden, Satan has been hell-bent on resisting God and his redemptive plans. And while I do not grasp it rationally, I do not think it irrational to accept that living with a holy passion, as 2 Peter 3:11-12 says, "hastens the day of his coming." Satan looks to delay. Let us look to hasten. And let us trust God concerning the mystery of it.

34. Bernard N. Nathanson, *Aborting America* (Doubleday, 1979)

35. Bernard N. Nathanson, *The Hand of God: A Journey from Death to Life by the Abortion Doctor Who Changed His Mind* (Regnery Publishing, 2001)

36. Bernard Nathanson, "Pro-Choice 1990," *New Dimensions,* October 1990, 38

37. David Aikman, *Jesus in Beijing: How Christianity is Transforming China and Changing the Global Balance of Power* (Regnery Publishing, 2006), 195-220

38. By contrast, the US currently suffers about 3,300 abortions a day, or 1.2 million a year. 2013 will mark 40 years of legalized abortion in America. During the first half, annual abortion rates climbed steadily to a high of 1.6 million in 1990. For the last 20 years, US abortions have steadily decreased. See ttp://www.abort73.com/abortion_facts/us_abortion_statistics/

39. All statistics and the original government resource available at http://www.allgirlsallowed.org/category/topics/forced-abortion

Wrestling with an Angel
A Story of Love, Disability and the Lessons of Grace

by Greg Lucas

The riveting, inspiring true story that readers have called "a touchstone book of my life," and "alternately hilarious and heartbreaking," a book that "turns the diamond of grace in such a way that you see facets you never really noticed before."

"C.S. Lewis wrote that he paradoxically loved *The Lord of the Rings* because it 'broke his heart'— and Greg Lucas' writing does the same for me."
Justin Taylor, Managing Editor, ESV Study Bible

"Witty... stunning... striking... humorous and heartfelt. *Wrestling with an Angel* provides a fresh, honest look at one father's struggle to embrace God in the midst of his son's disability. Can sheer laughter and weeping gracefully coexist in a world of so much affliction? Greg knows all about it. I highly recommend this wonderfully personal book!"
Joni Eareckson Tada, Joni and Friends International

"You will laugh; you will cry. You will feel sick; you will feel inspired. You will be repulsed by the ugliness of sin; you will be overwhelmed by the love of God. Greg Lucas takes us on an unforgettable ride as he extracts the most beautiful insights into grace from the most painful experiences of life."
David P. Murray, Puritan Reformed Theological Seminary

"Greg Lucas is a captivating storyteller. When he writes about life with Jake, I recognize God's grace and loving persistence in my life. I want more!"
Noël Piper, author, and wife of pastor and author John Piper

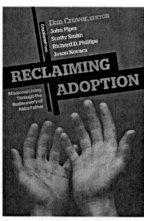

Reclaiming Adoption
Missional Living Through the
Rediscovery of Abba Father

Dan Cruver, Editor
John Piper, Scotty Smith
Richard D. Phillips, Jason Kovacs

"There is no greater need in our day than theological clarity. Dan has brought us near to God's heart. As you read this book, you will sense the need to embrace your own acceptance as God's adopted child."
Darrin Patrick, Pastor and author

"I can't recall ever hearing about, much less reading, a book like this before. Simply put, this remarkable volume fills a much-needed gap in our understanding of what the Bible says both about God's adoption of us and our adoption of others. I highly recommend it."
Sam Storms, *Author of* The Singing God: Discover the Joy of Being Enjoyed by God

"The authors writing here are some of the most fearless thinkers and activists in the Christian orphan care movement. Read. Be empowered. And then join Jesus for the orphans of the world."
Russell D. Moore, *Pastor and author* of Adopted for Life

"With spiritual insight and effective teaching, *Reclaiming Adoption* will help believers better understand our place with Christ and work in His kingdom."
Ed Stetzer, *President, LifeWay Research*

"Something like...a revival, is happening right now in evangelical theology....it may have the momentum to reinvigorate evangelical systematic theology....The most promising sign I've seen so far is the new book *Reclaiming Adoption.*
Fred Sanders, Ph.D., Faculty, Torrey Honors Institute, Biola University

The Organized Heart
A Woman's Guide to Conquering Chaos

by Staci Eastin

Disorganized?
You don't need more rules, the latest technique, or a new gadget.

This book will show you a different, better way. A way grounded in the grace of God.

"Staci Eastin packs a gracious punch, full of insights about our disorganized hearts and lives, immediately followed by the balm of gospel-shaped hopes. This book is ideal for accountability partners and small groups."

> *Carolyn McCulley, blogger, filmmaker, author of* Radical Womanhood *and* Did I Kiss Marriage Goodbye?

"Unless we understand the spiritual dimension of productivity, our techniques will ultimately backfire. Find that dimension here. Encouraging and uplifting rather than guilt-driven, this book can help women who want to be more organized but know that adding a new method is not enough."

> *Matt Perman, Director of Strategy at Desiring God, blogger, author of the forthcoming book,* What's Best Next: How the Gospel Transforms the Way You Get Things Done

"Organizing a home can be an insurmountable challenge for a woman. The Organized Heart makes a unique connection between idols of the heart and the ability to run a well-managed home. This is not a how-to. Eastin looks at sin as the root problem of disorganization. She offers a fresh new approach and one I recommend, especially to those of us who have tried all the other self-help models and failed."

> *Aileen Challies, Mom of three, and wife of blogger, author, and pastor Tim Challies*

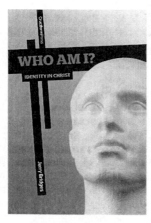

Who Am I?
Identity in Christ

by Jerry Bridges

Jerry Bridges unpacks Scripture to give the Christian eight clear, simple, interlocking answers to one of the most essential questions of life.

"Jerry Bridges' gift for simple but deep spiritual communication is fully displayed in this warm-hearted, biblical spelling out of the Christian's true identity in Christ."

> **J. I. Packer, *Theological Editor,* ESV Study Bible; *author,* Knowing God, A Quest for Godliness, Concise Theology**

"I know of no one better prepared than Jerry Bridges to write *Who Am I?* He is a man who knows who he is in Christ and he helps us to see succinctly and clearly who we are to be. Thank you for another gift to the Church of your wisdom and insight in this book."

> **R.C. Sproul, *founder, chairman, president, Ligonier Ministries; executive editor,* Tabletalk *magazine; general editor,* The Reformation Study Bible**

"*Who Am I?* answers one of the most pressing questions of our time in clear gospel categories straight from the Bible. This little book is a great resource to ground new believers and remind all of us of what God has made us through faith in Jesus. Thank the Lord for Jerry Bridges, who continues to provide the warm, clear, and biblically balanced teaching that has made him so beloved to this generation of Christians."

> **Richard D. Phillips, *Senior Minister, Second Presbyterian Church, Greenville, SC***

CPSIA information can be obtained
at www.ICGtesting.com
Printed in the USA
FFOW01n1541121015
17625FF